Questions Christians
Aren't Supposed to Ask

Questions Christians Aren't Supposed to Ask

James V. Brownson

WILLIAM B. EERDMANS PUBLISHING COMPANY
GRAND RAPIDS, MICHIGAN

Wm. B. Eerdmans Publishing Co.
4035 Park East Court SE, Grand Rapids, Michigan 49546
www.eerdmans.com

Published 2021
Printed in the United States of America

27 26 25 24 23 22 21   1 2 3 4 5 6 7

ISBN 978-0-8028-7841-0

Library of Congress Cataloging-in-Publication Data

Names: Brownson, James V., author.
Title: Questions Christians aren't supposed to ask / James V.
    Brownson.
Description: Grand Rapids, Michigan : William B. Eerdmans
    Publishing Company, 2021. | Includes bibliographical
    references and index. | Summary: "An exploration of
    several tough questions commonly asked about Christi-
    anity, each one addressed through a reading of specific
    biblical passages"—Provided by publisher.
Identifiers: LCCN 2020054723 | ISBN 9780802878410
    (paperback)
Subjects: LCSH: Apologetics. | Bible. New Testament—
    Criticism, interpretation, etc.
Classification: LCC BT1103 .B76 2021 | DDC 239—dc23
LC record available at https://lccn.loc.gov/2020054723

Contents

Introduction

This book focuses on the hard questions that younger people ask about Christianity and the church. I consulted with a wide range of young people to determine what were the most important questions to address, as they saw it. I selected the questions they thought were most important. But this book is written for those who love and care about these people rather than for the people asking the questions themselves. The reason for this is fairly simple: younger people asking these sorts of questions are probably not going to buy books to address their questions. But their parents and friends may well do so!

There is a second reason for the intended audience. I'm a New Testament scholar, and for each question, rather than trying to find a comprehensive answer, I explore a specific biblical text, to see how it both reframes and refocuses the question, but also how, at least to some extent, it answers the question. Those without a certain reverence for Scripture may not find these biblical explorations worthwhile, but their family and friends might. So it is this latter group that I have kept in mind as I have written this book. I hope you find it helpful!

1 ǁ Hypocrisy

If there is so much hypocrisy in the church, why should I believe and join it?

ǁ *Matthew 6:1–6*

It doesn't take detailed analysis to recognize the various forms of hypocrisy that permeate Christian religious organizations today. Christians from many different walks of life are concerned about some issues but tend to be oblivious to (or at least less sensitive to) other issues. Conservative Christians radically oppose gay marriage, but sometimes they don't seem nearly as worried about the sexual misconduct of the straight people in their own churches (including such obvious problems as divorce and remarriage, addressed explicitly in a variety of texts) or sometimes even the misbehavior of their own leaders. Progressive Christians often work hard to oppose the death penalty but can sometimes seem far less concerned about the death of babies through abortion. In these cases, public positions easily seen by others are clearly in view—exactly what Jesus addresses in Matthew. Lots of people in our culture worry about these issues. This chapter will explore Matthew 6:1–6, to see how it addresses the question at the beginning of the chapter.

[1] "Beware of practicing your piety before others in order to be seen by them; for then you have no reward from your Father in heaven.

[2] "So whenever you give alms, do not sound a trumpet before you, as the hypocrites do in the synagogues and in the streets, so that they may be praised by others. Truly I tell you, they have received their reward. [3] But when you give alms, do not let your left hand know what your right hand is doing, [4] so that your alms may be done in secret; and your Father who sees in secret will reward you.

[5] "And whenever you pray, do not be like the hypocrites; for they love to stand and pray in the synagogues and at the street corners, so that they may be seen by others. Truly I tell you, they have received their reward. [6] But whenever you pray, go into your room and shut the door and pray to your Father who is in secret; and your Father who sees in secret will reward you."

If we are to make sense of Matthew 6 and its particular focus on hypocrisy, we need to begin by looking at the original meaning of the word "hypocrite." In early Greek usage (long before the time of Jesus), this word was used neutrally of an "orator," or even more commonly, of an "actor." By the time the New Testament was written, however, the meaning of the word had turned decidedly negative. A "hypocrite" was still an actor, as in earlier literature, but now more particularly in the sense of a *pretender*, or *dissembler*. The word was rarely used during the New Testament period in an explicitly theatrical sense but almost always in a general, more negative sense. Its focus falls on the gap between someone's true identity and the identity the person is projecting at any particular moment. The central problem for hypocrites in the New Testament period was thus the *loss of a coherent identity*, and an increase in behavior directed to specific people in search of specific sorts of praise or commendation, rather than the pursuit of an authentic identity.

This is the understanding of hypocrisy that dominates the New Testament and, to a large extent, contemporary thinking as well. Religion becomes hypocritical particularly when certain religious behaviors can be used to increase one's public status. We see this pattern clearly in a text such as Matthew 6:1–6. Twice in this passage, Jesus warns against acting like "the hypocrites" (vv. 2 and 5). He speaks of hypocrisy in conjunction with specific religious practices: almsgiving and praying. In each case, Jesus emphasizes that the primary concern of hypocrites is really the attempt to win the favor of others. In each case, he says, "Truly I tell you, they have received their reward." One might translate more literally, "Truly I tell you, they get their pay." The reward/pay, of course, is the approval of others (rather than the claimed religious motive of divine approval).

So here is the heart of hypocrisy, for Jesus. People engage in ostensibly religious behaviors such as almsgiving and prayer that appear to have God as their object and goal. However, in reality, the object and goal is public status. As Jesus sees it, people engage in the public exercise of religious practices in order to gain public status. According to Jesus, when people do this, "they get their pay"; they receive the public status they are pursuing, and any further soliciting of divine approval is essentially irrelevant. A religious practice is engaged, but the real reasons for the practice are not at all religious; the focus is instead on public approval.

One might question whether, particularly in a Western, postreligious culture like ours, this would continue to be a problem. Religious behaviors do not grant persons the same broad public status today that they did in previous eras. But Western, postreligious culture does consist of interest groups that do have specifically religious interests and values. Thus, whereas some religious practices may not gain a person broad social status within the culture as a whole, they may enhance social status within a specific, more religiously oriented group. This is not unlike the situation faced by Jesus himself. The Roman occupiers of Judea and Galilee would have had little interest in the religious behaviors Jesus was talking about, and those behaviors would have gained their practitioners no status in the eyes of the Roman occupiers. But among the religious leadership, such religious behaviors were clearly valued, and enacting them would cause one to be held in high regard, reinforcing the temptation to hypocrisy that Jesus spoke about.

Thus, for Jesus, the core problem with hypocrisy focuses upon motives. Explicitly religious behaviors such as prayer and almsgiving may proceed from nonreligious motives; those doing them seek approval from particular groups rather than divine sanction or blessing. In such cases, people "get their pay" quite apart from any divine response at all.

Finally, the problem of religious hypocrisy arises in a more pronounced way, particularly when religious groups lose focus on clear and coherent motives, when public approval replaces deeper religious motives for behavior. Jesus saw this happening in his day, and we see similar dynamics operating in many religious groups today. It's not that the motives for various groups engaging in public advocacy are wrong, in their view. Pro-life groups genuinely believe that babies should not be killed in the womb. Groups opposing gay marriage genuinely believe that marriage should be between a man and a woman. Social justice advocacy groups genuinely believe in their cause.

The problem arises when those motives are not coherently and consistently lived out. Pro-life groups don't seem, particularly to their opponents, to be as worried about the death of criminals and other marginalized populations. Groups opposing gay marriage seem to pick and choose which issues in sexual ethics to focus on. Social justice advocates seem, again to outsiders, to decide, at least sometimes in a seemingly arbitrary way, which issues are important. This loss of coherence and consistency of practice is one of the surest signs that hypocrisy is a problem, and people need to recognize and acknowledge these problems.

Another sign of this loss of coherent and consistent motives is when public approval looms large. According to Jesus, public approval is almost always the sign of incoherent or corrupted motives, particularly in the religious sphere. In fact, Jesus urges his followers to adopt religious practices where public approval is not even an option, where praying and almsgiving occur only in secret and are rewarded only by the God who sees in secret. Twice Jesus repeats, "and your Father who sees in secret will reward you" (Matt. 6:4b, 6b).

What is at stake here is the difference between human approval and divine approval. When human approval appears as a motive for religious actions, hypocrisy is almost always present, regardless of how worthy the apparently divinely directed practice may be. What this means, of course, is that religious groups, if they want to follow Jesus, must steadfastly avoid postures of public approval or disapproval for religiously motivated behaviors. For if they engage in such approaches, they almost invariably subject their participants to the potential of conflicted motives and hypocrisy, implicitly encouraging them to seek human approval under the guise of behaviors that ostensibly seek divine approval.

So, at least from the perspective of Jesus, the complaint about hypocrisy that this chapter focuses upon is an entirely legitimate one, and in fact, is a perennial danger of religious groups. If it was such a problem in Jesus's day, it is not surprising that it continues to arise today. At the same time, if the founder of Christianity warns against the practice of hypocrisy, then those Christian groups that seek to follow him must confront their own tendencies to hypocrisy and attempt to root such tendencies out of their practices. Hence, ironically, those who object to hypocrisy in the church may be more sensitive to the founder of Christian faith than those who claim to be his followers.

One more point about this text needs to be underscored. Matthew 6 is concerned with religious practices that were common sources of hypocrisy in Jesus's day: almsgiving and prayer. However, these are not the only places where hypocrisy becomes a problem. The NRSV translation of Matthew 6:1 states, "Beware of practicing

your piety before others in order to be seen by them."
But the word rendered "piety" could just as readily be
translated "righteousness." This is clearly *not* a negative
word in Matthew. In Matthew 3:15, Jesus himself states
that he must be baptized "to fulfill all righteousness." In
5:6 he pronounces a blessing on those who "hunger and
thirst for righteousness." In 5:20 he declares that the righteousness of his followers must exceed that of the scribes
and Pharisees. In 6:33, the disciples are instructed to seek
God's kingdom *and God's righteousness.*

Righteousness for Matthew is clearly a good thing. But
even a good thing can be corrupted, and this is what is in
view in Matthew 6:1–6. Behaviors and practices that were
originally divinely oriented for human beings can become
a focus for public approval rather than divine approval.
When that happens, even specifically religious practices
and concerns quickly lose their meaning. So the question
of motives is a persistently urgent one, and the problem
of hypocrisy is often evident, particularly when we see
inconsistency between public behavior and private behavior, or excessive subgroup affirmation of certain public
behaviors, leaving out other, more private behaviors from
the picture.

So, if there is so much hypocrisy in the church, why
should I and those I may love believe and join it? We
are not the first ones to ask this question. It goes back
to Jesus himself and is a perennial problem for religious
groups. But the answer is not found in the avoidance of
religion but rather in a deeper embrace of the teaching of
Jesus himself, who warns against the appeal of the hypocrites and invites us into a deeper and more coherent
way of living.

Discussion Questions

- Do you agree with the perspective on hypocrisy presented here?
- Is the problem with "public positions" outlined in this essay part of your experience? In what ways?
- Is hypocrisy defined in the social/political way of this chapter more of a problem to you than hypocrisy defined as moral behavior in personal living that is preached but not practiced?
- How widely affirmed do behaviors need to be in order for them to be an incentive to hypocrisy?
- Do you agree with the author that "those who object to hypocrisy in the church may be more sensitive to the founder of Christian faith than those who claim to be his followers"?
- Is this a problem for the right *and* the left wings of the church, as this chapter attempts to argue?

For Further Exploration

Bruner, Frederick Dale. *Matthew: A Commentary*. Vol. 1, *The Christbook: Matthew 1–12*. Revised and expanded ed. Grand Rapids: Eerdmans, 2004. Pages 281–88.

Powery, Emerson. "Hypocrisy, Hypocrite." In *The New Interpreter's Dictionary of the Bible*, vol. 2. Nashville: Abingdon, 2007.

2 ⫼ Hope

If Christians, like me, want to see
a better world, why aren't they
moving in the same direction?

⫼ Romans 8:19–25

In our American context, everyone wants to see a better world. To quote the Declaration of Independence, we all long for a deeper experience of "life, liberty, and the pursuit of happiness." However, there are profound disagreements about what that better world looks like, and how we should move toward it. Is it essentially free-market capitalism that moves us toward that better world, or is it the formulation of government policies and standards that shape and direct the interactions of citizens? Should the laws of the nation reflect specific moral frameworks on controversial topics such as abortion, prostitution, marriage, and marijuana usage, or should individuals be allowed to decide these issues on the basis of their own moral framework? How should the government determine the balance between the values of freedom, morality, and justice, or, to quote again from the Declaration of Independence, what is the best way to "life, liberty, and the pursuit of happiness"?

Unfortunately, disagreements on these topics are pervasive in American society, and these disagreements also

occur among Christians. In this chapter, we will explore
Romans 8:19–25, not so much for answers to this question but more to see how the biblical text reframes and
refocuses the way we think about a question like this.

Here is the text from Romans 8:

> [19] For the creation waits with eager longing for the re-
> vealing of the children of God; [20] for the creation was
> subjected to futility, not of its own will but by the will
> of the one who subjected it, in hope [21] that the creation
> itself will be set free from its bondage to decay and
> will obtain the freedom of the glory of the children
> of God. [22] We know that the whole creation has been
> groaning in labor pains until now; [23] and not only the
> creation, but we ourselves, who have the first fruits
> of the Spirit, groan inwardly while we wait for adop-
> tion, the redemption of our bodies. [24] For in hope we
> were saved. Now hope that is seen is not hope. For who
> hopes for what is seen? [25] But if we hope for what we
> do not see, we wait for it with patience.

Observe how the passage speaks of "the creation." The
word "creation" occurs in each of the first five verses of
our text. "Creation" is clearly a central component of Romans 8. In essence, then, to take this text seriously, we
cannot fail to take seriously the creation, or more specifically, the material world. We cannot fail to look for its
redemption. In Genesis 1, we see how God separates the
various elements of creation—light and darkness, land
and sea—and then populates land and sea with plants,
animals, fish, birds, and people. God pronounces that
all this was "good." Of course, this is quickly followed in

the narrative by the account of the Fall in Genesis 3, and the subsequent cursing of the ground in Genesis 3:17–18. Romans 8:20 picks up this language of the Fall when it declares that "the creation was subjected to futility." The Romans text goes on to affirm the conviction that "the creation itself will be set free from its bondage to decay and will obtain the freedom of the glory of the children of God." So, from a Christian perspective, the "better world" that our chapter's question longs for is a material world—a redeemed creation.

Yet this is not always clearly seen in some Christian circles. Some circles emphasize so strongly the heavenly destiny of believers that their relationship to the material world is seen as only transitory and having no final significance. Instead, the focus falls almost exclusively on "spiritual" matters. This is sometimes coupled with an avoidance of creational issues, under the rubric of claims such as "This world is not my home." But the focus on creation in this text won't let Christians get away with these sorts of claims.

Neither will the doctrine of the incarnation permit this sort of stance. The claim that the second person of the Trinity "became flesh and lived among us" (John 1:14), as well as the early Christian affirmation of the "resurrection *of the body*" in texts such as the Apostles' Creed, makes any disparagement of the material world a deeply problematic posture for Christians to adopt. It simply will not do to assert, "This world is not my home," and to use such a claim as an excuse to avoid difficult questions surrounding care for the creation. The material world matters, and care for the material world is an unavoidable dimension of Christian ethics, both now and in eternity.

But this certainly does not settle the question of a "better world," in and of itself. Many Christians agree that God cares about the creation, and that we should care about it as well. This agreement is profoundly important, but it does not entirely settle the issue. Christians may still disagree profoundly about how such care for the creation should shape our lives, to say nothing of how it should shape governmental policies. Yet this disagreement affects very tangibly and concretely the "better world" of which our question speaks, and reflects deep disagreements about how we are to move toward such a "better world." As important as this initial agreement about materiality may be, it is not enough merely to affirm the goodness of creation, in the midst of profound disagreements about how we are to move more deeply toward such goodness, particularly involving issues like justice, freedom, and the government's involvement in issues of morality.

Also assumed in this passage is the affirmation that the future of humans and the future of the creation are inextricably intertwined. We cannot separate a vision for the future of humans from a vision for the future of the creation. But perhaps the most significant implication of this fact is that humans are envisioned *corporately*, and not just individualistically, just as the creation is envisioned in its totality, not only in various particularities. All the references to human beings in this passage are in the plural, not in the singular. Here we confront one of the powerful forces in contemporary society that affects the "better world" we envision: the inclination to individualism. For many folks, the question of a "better world" focuses on what is better for individuals, and what is better for individuals is understood to be necessarily better for society and the world as a whole. As a result of this individualism, the bias tilts toward an ethic of freedom—the capacity for individuals to do whatever they deem best.

But the first mention of "freedom" in our Romans text refers not to the freedom of individuals but to the freedom of the creation, in Romans 8:21. The creation will be set free from "its bondage to decay" and thereby "obtain the freedom of the glory of the children of God." The "bondage to decay" from which the creation is freed is the result of the Fall, not merely the actions of individuals. It is systemic in character. But Paul envisions a future in which this systemic dimension of the creation is transformed, and where the redemption begun in Christ and seen in Christians will someday extend to the whole of the creation, envisioned corporately. Indeed, the redemptive work that God is accomplishing in Christ cannot be complete without this reality.

But even this fact does not deliver us entirely from the individualistic/corporate identity debate. Our text describes the corporate freedom of the creation as flowing from "the freedom of the glory of the children of God." So, what begins in the church, among the "children of God," eventually flows out into the creation as a whole. This presupposes, of course, a distinction between the church and society as a whole, and a starting point for the new creation, not in society as a whole but in the church. But even this starting point of the church should not lead us into a modern notion of individualism. Indeed, even the church is, in its essence, a corporate, rather than an individualistic, reality, even though it is not the same as the larger society as a whole. So we must at least attempt to engage the "better world" question not merely in an individualistic way but by envisioning a corporate dimension of such a world that begins in the church and moves toward the whole world.

Moreover, if we begin with the church, we also begin with the church's identity "in Christ." According to verse 23, the church waits "for adoption, the redemption of our bodies." The church waits for its full identity as children of God to emerge—an identity rooted and grounded in Christ, who is supremely the child of God. The church waits for the redemption of our bodies, because the body of Jesus himself was redeemed in the resurrection, and we wait for the same reality to be fully manifested in those who belong to Christ.

So the "better world" of which our question speaks emerges in stages. To be sure, the material world is in view, not just a spiritual world. And this world is presented corporately and not just individualistically. But the transformation of this world does not occur all at once; it occurs in stages. One way to understand these stages focuses on proximity to Christ, who stands at the center of God's plan for transformation. It is in those who are closest to Christ (that is, in the church) that we see the clearest beginnings of the transformation that is finally destined to encompass the whole world. The church exists not as an escape from the world but as the starting point for the transformation, not just of itself but of the whole world.

But there is one more way in which this view that transformation occurs in stages manifests itself, and that is found in a more temporal perspective. The restoration of creation is nowhere nearly complete yet. Its final restoration continues to be a matter of hope, something we do not yet see in anything like its fullness. We see this particularly in verses 24–25 of our passage, which speak of the "hope" in which we were saved and for which we wait with patience.

This focus on hope brings two additional dimensions to the Christian quest for a better world. On the one hand, it encourages the cultivation of a big and comprehensive vision. It refuses to allow a pragmatism about what is and is not possible to cloud the vision of a transformed creation. This vision is willing to endure the absence of "practicalities" that might be required in a much shorter time frame of transformation. This is not a hope only of what is seen, but as Paul says, of what we do not see. What is more, this hope refuses to be daunted by those things that seem to be the limitations of the present. There is a kind of pragmatism that stands as the very opposite of Christian hope, worried always about how a vision for transformation can be implemented in the foreseeable future. Christian hope embraces a larger picture, a wider time frame, and a transcendent power that accomplishes the transformation of the world. It waits for that reality with a deep and abiding patience, because it already sees the end and goal in the crucified and risen Messiah.

Of course, none of these observations completely settles the matter of the nature of the "better world" envisioned by Christians, nor the processes by which we move toward that better world. This chapter does not attempt to resolve these disputes. However, the text we have explored invites a new set of questions for Christians to consider as they struggle together with the nature of the "better world" envisioned by the gospel, and the steps required to move toward that world: How does the "better world" envisioned by Christians encompass the material creation? How does it engage humanity, not merely as individuals, but corporately? How is it grounded in Christ himself, and how is that a big enough vision to require nothing short of the power of God to be fully achieved? And finally, how do we live in a hope that can energize and sustain us in this vision, as we wait for that future with patience? These questions will help to shape a Christian conversation so that it may proceed more productively.

Discussion Questions

- What do you think is the most productive path to hope?
- Is this path to hope marked by greater freedom, or clearer laws, or both?
- How well, and in what ways, does Romans 8:19–25 speak to this problem?
- Do you agree with the author that emphasizing the heavenly destiny of believers vis-à-vis their relationship to the material world is a problem for Christians?
- Is excessive individualism a problem in America? Why or why not?
- This chapter makes a lot of the link between the creation and the material universe. Do you agree or disagree, and why?
- What are some of the new questions this chapter raises for you?

For Further Exploration

Brueggemann, Walter. *Reality, Grief, Hope: Three Urgent Prophetic Tasks*. Grand Rapids: Eerdmans, 2014.

Fitzmyer, Joseph A. *Romans: A New Translation with Introduction and Commentary*. New York: Doubleday, 1993. Pages 504–15.

Hiebert, Theodore. "Creation." In *New Interpreter's Dictionary of the Bible*, vol. 1. Nashville: Abingdon, 2006.

Levenson, Jon D. *Creation and the Persistence of Evil: The Jewish Drama of Divine Omnipotence*. San Francisco: Harper & Row, 1988. Pages 3–50.

3 ǁ *Pain*

*Why should anyone believe in God
in a world with so much pain?*

ǁ *Mark 8:31–38*

This question proceeds from classic discussions of the
"problem of evil." This discussion in the Christian tradition carries with it a number of important assumptions
that need to be clearly in our minds. Significant parts of
this tradition assume, first of all, that God is omnipotent.
This means that *all* the pain we see and experience in the
world must have some specific divine purpose or reason.
Otherwise, an omnipotent God would not allow this sort
of experience to happen.

But it seems to be an impossible task to discern the
purpose and reason for all the pain and suffering in the
world. Some say that belief in divine omnipotence needs
simply to be embraced, despite this difficulty. However,
for many people, even those we love, this is not a viable
option, and the alternative is simply to render belief in the
God portrayed by the Christian tradition as impossible.

This problem is addressed in Mark 8:31–38.

³¹ Then he began to teach them that the Son of Man
must undergo great suffering, and be rejected by the
elders, the chief priests, and the scribes, and be killed,

and after three days rise again. ³²He said all this quite openly. And Peter took him aside and began to rebuke him. ³³But turning and looking at his disciples, he rebuked Peter and said, "Get behind me, Satan! For you are setting your mind not on divine things but on human things."

³⁴He called the crowd with his disciples, and said to them, "If any want to become my followers, let them deny themselves and take up their cross and follow me. ³⁵For those who want to save their life will lose it, and those who lose their life for my sake, and for the sake of the gospel, will save it. ³⁶For what will it profit them to gain the whole world and forfeit their life? ³⁷Indeed, what can they give in return for their life? ³⁸Those who are ashamed of me and of my words in this adulterous and sinful generation, of them the Son of Man will also be ashamed when he comes in the glory of his Father with the holy angels."

The God who speaks through the words of Jesus in Mark 8:31–38 hardly seems to be omnipotent, at least in a simplistic sense of the word. Here Jesus speaks of a great suffering. How or why would such a God speak of his/her own suffering? How can an omnipotent God "undergo great suffering," particularly when omnipotence grants the ability to correct whatever it is that causes pain? Why would God suffer, when this same God has an omnipotent ability to alter the circumstances that cause suffering in the first place? And if God does not use omnipotence to correct circumstances that cause divine suffering, then what is the purpose of omnipotence in the first place? This text doesn't speak directly to the notion of "omnipotence," and it doesn't use the term, but it seems clearly to presuppose that at least some areas lie outside of any notion of direct divine control or omnipotence. The God portrayed here seems scarcely to be omnipotent. Otherwise, why would the Son of Man need to suffer at all?

But this is not the end of our dilemma. For if God is not omnipotent, then another version of our chapter's question immediately arises: If God can't fix the pain of the world, why should we believe in, or worship, such a God? It may well be that the God portrayed in Scripture is not omnipotent, and that this God can't simply erase much of the suffering in the world. However, if the God of the Bible cannot correct the pain in the world, because this God is not able to do so, at least in any direct way, then that hardly seems more attractive than an omnipotent God who refuses to correct the pain of the world. Pain persists, and God can do nothing about it. Why should anyone believe in or worship such a God, particularly when one of the benefits of such a belief— protection from unnecessary pain and suffering—seems to be out of the picture? These questions are widespread in our culture.

So the pain of the world looms large when one is thinking about God. Either God is omnipotent, and we cannot explain the pain of the world, or God is not omnipotent, and is therefore of little use in counteracting the pain of the world. Either way, the pain of the world raises significant questions about belief in God.

Yet I can think of at least one reason to pay attention to the way our text from Mark speaks to the question of this chapter. Why should we believe in God in a world with so much pain? Because the God of the Bible as present in Jesus of Nazareth knows and shares that pain. This stands in radical contrast to a simplistic notion of omnipotence. In a simplistic world, the only appropriate posture, when we encounter pain, is simply to let go of our pain, or to realize, first with our heads, and eventually with our hearts, that divine omnipotence means that this pain must have some reason, even if we cannot see or discern what that reason might be. Either pain is an illusion that must be abandoned, or it is necessary and must be embraced without complaint, whether we understand it or not.

However, if God himself suffers as we see in Christ, it suggests that our pain may be entirely legitimate, not simply the result of a misunderstanding or an illusion. This becomes clearer when we begin to contemplate alternative ways of looking at our world and the denial of God's existence. For if God does not exist or is irrelevant to our pain, then pain and anguish exist simply to be avoided as much as possible. This becomes a particularly complex notion when we inject into the mix the realities of power and resources. Those who have power or resources in this world will succeed the most in avoiding or eliminating pain, and the pain of others exists not to be sympathized with but to be avoided.

But if there is a God, and this God embraces our pain and feels it along with us, then something else is going on that we must pay attention to here. The most powerful being does not avoid or eliminate pain, nor does that being completely overcome pain, but rather experiences it together with the rest of the creation. This is the God of the Bible, the God portrayed in Jesus in our text. This suggests that the biblical world is a world in which compassion plays a much larger role than we often assume.

In our human context, we tend to see compassion in a way that focuses on our most intimate relationships. But in the biblical world, compassion is not simply a concern for those closest to you, whom you may be able to assist in their pain. Rather, compassion is a universal perspective, grounded in the divine disposition toward the world itself.

Yet this does not yet resolve all our dilemmas either. Does this virtue of divinely ordained compassion accomplish anything beyond simply magnifying our suffering and anguish over the pain, not only of those closest to us but of the entire world? Is it a virtue to suffer more, when nothing can be done to stop the suffering that grieves us in the first place? Here's where the final verse of our text (v. 38) comes into play: "Those who are ashamed of me and of my words in this adulterous and sinful generation, of them the Son of Man will also be ashamed when he comes in the glory of his Father with the holy angels." Jesus speaks here not only of the compassion of God but also of the judgment of God. God may not be omnipotent in an absolute sense, but this God does act in judgment upon those who disobey. The text announces this impending judgment.

This is the God of this passage: very powerful but not omnipotent, at least in a simplistic sense of that word; deeply compassionate but not hamstrung in the midst of pain and sorrow; endlessly creative in moving the world toward the divine goals, amidst a deep sense of justice. This is also the God who has come to us in Jesus Christ, whom Christians proclaim as the incarnate one. Although Jesus displayed extraordinary power in his ministry— healing the sick, expelling demons, walking on water, feeding the hungry, and many other such things—he also speaks in our text of the ways in which he suffered the humiliation of crucifixion, and cried out on the cross, "My God, my God, why have you forsaken me?" The incarnate one had great power but also knew deeply the reality of anguish and pain.

So, why should we believe in God, in a world with so much pain? Because the alternatives (an omnipotent God or no God) are even worse. With an omnipotent God, pain is either an illusion or a sign of divine absence. Why should anyone worship such a God? But if there is no God, then we are in another sort of dilemma, because the only answer to pain is then the application of power and resources, and the world will endlessly struggle with the limitations that various people face in accessing that power and those resources. Injustice and inequity seem the inevitable result, with no easy solution in sight.

But we don't believe in such a God simply because the alternatives are worse. The God of the Bible also shows a mysterious path forward, in the midst of a painful world, where compassion and suffering have a surprisingly large significance. Not all our questions are answered; not all our dilemmas are resolved. But because the God of the Bible is a God of deep compassion, we are invited to the strange posture of a compassionate vision of the world.

This compassion is simply naive, if a simplistic notion of omnipotence is a reality. Why show compassion on those who are experiencing pain because God wills it? To do so is to act against the will of God—never a good idea! But if the alternative vision is true, and God simply does not exist, then compassion is a waste of time. The only thing that matters is eliminating or diminishing the pain and suffering that you may experience, or that those close to you may be undergoing. Anything beyond this is, at least usually, a luxury we cannot afford.

But if we take seriously the God portrayed in this text, and in the rest of the Bible, then divine love and compassion move to the center of the picture. We are still left with unanswered questions about why pain exists in the world. But the answer to these questions lies neither in negating our questions nor in abandoning belief in God. Rather, the answer is found in trusting that God is not finished yet. God is extremely powerful but not omnipotent in a simplistic sense. We are invited to trust that this God is not yet finished with the world and will ultimately draw all things into harmony with the divine purposes. And even the worst experiences of pain that seem entirely irrational acquire new significance, in light of the God-forsakenness of the incarnate one. We don't have answers, but we know whom to trust.

Discussion Questions

- How do the perspectives on pain rendered in this chapter resonate with you?
- What is your understanding of divine omnipotence, and is this a problem as this chapter discusses it? Why or why not?
- Why do you believe Jesus needed to suffer and die, and be raised from the dead?
- Which is a more severe problem for you? The claim that God is omnipotent, or the denial of that claim?

- What do you make of the argument made in this chapter that the alternatives to divine omnipotence are worse? Do you agree or disagree?

For Further Exploration

Hart, David Bentley. *The Doors of the Sea: Where Was God in the Tsunami?* Grand Rapids: Eerdmans, 2005.

Hasker, William. *The Triumph of God over Evil: Theodicy for a World of Suffering.* Downers Grove, IL: IVP Academic, 2008.

Lane, William L. *The Gospel of Mark.* New International Commentary on the New Testament. Grand Rapids: Eerdmans, 1974. Pages 294–311.

Levenson, Jon D. *Creation and the Persistence of Evil: The Jewish Drama of Divine Omnipotence.* San Francisco: Harper & Row, 1988. Pages 53–127.

Rice, Richard. *Suffering and the Search for Meaning: Contemporary Responses to the Problem of Pain.* Downers Grove, IL: IVP Academic, 2014.

4 ⫽ Politics

*Why should I become a Christian
when I find the public agenda of
many Christians so offensive?*

⫽ Matthew 22:15–22

The present public tone in the USA is one of the most
highly polarized politically that anyone has seen for quite
a long time. We are seeing a new phenomenon, in which
politicians are motivated to stir up the deepest sorts of
passions to motivate their bases, regardless of how those
passions may alienate others. We saw this operate in strik-
ing ways in the 2016 election. White evangelical voters
voted for Trump in that election at a rate of at least 80
percent, while other minorities, even those of an evangelical persuasion, voted strongly in the opposite direction.
Given that the Trump presidency has also been among
the most controversial in recent memory, it is not surprising that people are asking the above question.

The recent death of evangelist Billy Graham has
brought up many of these questions afresh. Billy himself
paid a price for his close association with Richard Nixon,
particularly after the demise of the Nixon administration,
and his son Franklin Graham, who has taken over the
helm of the Graham empire, has certainly been among

the most provocative figures politically, advocating a very strong right-wing agenda.

But before we dive into all the immediate political questions raised by these people and events, it's worth stepping back to a somewhat broader question, about the relationship between Christian faith and politics more generally. That's where the Scripture text on which this chapter will focus comes into play: Matthew 22:15–22, with its focus upon paying taxes.

> [15] Then the Pharisees went and plotted to entrap him in what he said. [16] So they sent their disciples to him, along with the Herodians, saying, "Teacher, we know that you are sincere, and teach the way of God in accordance with truth, and show deference to no one; for you do not regard people with partiality. [17] Tell us, then, what you think. Is it lawful to pay taxes to the emperor, or not?" [18] But Jesus, aware of their malice, said, "Why are you putting me to the test, you hypocrites? [19] Show me the coin used for the tax." And they brought him a denarius. [20] Then he said to them, "Whose head is this, and whose title?" [21] They answered, "The emperor's." Then he said to them, "Give therefore to the emperor the things that are the emperor's, and to God the things that are God's." [22] When they heard this, they were amazed; and they left him and went away.

Jesus's ministry occurred in a country under Roman control. Israel/Palestine had experienced brief periods of freedom after the return of the Israelites from exile, but this freedom came to an end in 63 BC, when Rome conquered Jerusalem and placed the country under Roman rule. Beginning at that time, local leadership in Judea was engaged in a difficult juggling act, trying to give Rome—the occupying power—what it wanted while maintaining contact and sympathy with a population that deeply resented Roman rule. King Herod the Great, who was king in Judea at the birth of Jesus, exemplifies this tension. On the one hand, he rebuilt the temple and encouraged the further development of Israel's distinctive religious identity. But he also was closely allied with Roman rule, and his attempt to kill the infant Jesus as a messianic threat exemplifies his paranoia and obsession with power (see Matt. 2).

So the question posed to Jesus about paying taxes to Caesar is a loaded one. The different groups in Judea at that time would have offered very different answers to it. On the one hand, groups like the Zealots were engaged in active military opposition to Rome. It is hard to imagine that people willing to put their lives on the line in resistance to Rome would advocate paying taxes to the same Roman Empire. On the other hand, those whose power was closely linked to the temple and the Jerusalem establishment would want to keep Rome happy and would gladly pay taxes, in exchange for the relative freedom and empowerment that this posture brought to them in particular.

However, not only is the *question* posed to Jesus a complicated one; Jesus's *answer* is also complicated: "Give therefore to the emperor the things that are the emperor's, and to God the things that are God's." At one level, everything belongs to God, and Jesus's statement, at least by this interpretation, seems to speak against paying taxes. The text presupposes, at the very least, a "trump card" (no pun intended) that may give Christians, at least under some circumstances, the freedom, or perhaps even the obligation, to act in civil disobedience, including even not paying their taxes (cf. Acts 5:29, "We must obey God rather than any human authority"). In the centuries following the beginning of Christian faith, one of the primary ways the gospel was spread was through the witness of martyrs whom the Roman Empire killed for their faith, martyrs such as Justin Martyr and Polycarp, to name just two. Opposition to Rome and embrace of the Christian faith were often seen by early Christians as two sides of the same coin, and following someone Rome had crucified made perfect sense in this framework. One can readily imagine such martyrdom being accompanied by a resistance to the paying of taxes to Rome. Why should Christians finance the government that kills their leaders?

At another level, some interpreters of Matthew 22:15–22 may be inclined to suggest that money is a "human" reality rather than one that proceeds from God, and that therefore Jesus was advocating paying taxes to Caesar. This would be supported by Jesus's note that the image and title of the emperor are on the coin, and that therefore the emperor has some claim to the coin, and thus, there must be some recognized right of the government to demand the payment of taxes. This is reflected in texts like Romans 13:7, which calls its readers to pay "taxes to whom taxes are due." Indeed, one can scarcely imagine the emergence of Christianity in the city of Rome, the center of the empire, without a willingness by Christian Roman citizens to pay their taxes.

Both of these lines of emphasis occur at various points in Christian history. Martyrdom and resistance took prominence in the early centuries of Christian faith, and support for paying taxes emerged strongly after the conversion of Constantine in the fourth century. But at various points in Christian history, these two lines persist in various ways, particularly when governments adopt positions that either favor or denigrate the place of Christians.

Both streams are also present in the current American democratic context. Here part of the reason people pay taxes is to ensure justice and equity—values deeply embedded in both the American and the Christian traditions—but disagreements regarding how government should implement these values are embedded in the system as well, leading some to resist paying taxes.

So our present American context is not the first one in which people reacted against the political inclinations of others, and sometimes attached certain political positions to Christian faith. This goes all the way back to the early church, and ultimately to the ambiguity of Jesus's pronouncement itself. The problem of disagreements over the political agenda of Christians is not new.

One thing the question at the head of this chapter does allude to is that Christians *themselves* often disagree over politics. Rarely is there only one "Christian" political position. These disagreements include both the relative ranking of goals toward which the political process should be directed and the best means to achieve those ends. Take, for example, the relative importance of justice and liberty, particularly in relation to each other. Some Christians believe that the best means to achieve justice is the preservation of liberty and the freedom of individuals. Other Christians, who do not disparage the importance of liberty, believe that justice is best achieved by some limitations on the absolute practice of liberty. In particular, these Christians often emphasize the need for the privileged to give up some of their liberty to aid the lives of those who suffer and are oppressed. Thus, there are radically divergent views of the role of government in achieving justice among Christians. Some Christians see government as the means to greater justice, while others see government as part of the problem and regard liberty as the radical limitation of the role of government. This, of course, results in radically different political positions and substantial disagreement among Christians in the political sphere.

But it is precisely at this point that Christians may be able to bring something fresh to the table of political disagreement. Christians have had, from the beginning of the faith, as part of its ethos, a radical summons to pay attention to and to listen carefully to those they disagree with. We see this play itself out in the early chapters of the book of Acts, where Christians disagreed over whether gentiles should be expected to observe the entire Jewish law, including things like Sabbath observance, kosher eating, and circumcision. Indeed, these disagreements culminated in the Council of Jerusalem in Acts 15, where supposedly the issues were hammered out. But one doesn't need to read too far into the letters of Paul before one realizes that even after this "council," disagreements persisted.

Here is where Paul's discourse starts to become very interesting. In his letter to the Romans, Paul calls for a posture of tolerance and patience with those who may take a more conservative position on the Jewish law. In Romans 15:1, he declares, "We who are strong ought to put up with the failings of the weak, and not to please ourselves." On the one hand, Paul characterizes his own position as the "strong" one, clearly assuming its superiority to other views. This is not a perspective that minimizes these differences as immaterial. On the other hand, Paul clearly calls for patience, understanding, and acceptance to be exercised toward those who take other positions on the relative importance of the Jewish law for gentile Christians (consider the discussion in Romans 14, for example).

I wonder whether the same sort of generosity might be commended to Christians today who find themselves in disagreements about political agendas. On the one hand, this is not to assume that all political disagreements between Christians are insubstantial: there are "strong" positions and there are "weak" positions. Christians may also, of course, differ (as they no doubt did in Paul's day) over which positions are "strong" and which are "weak."

But Christians, regardless of whom they regard as the "strong" or the "weak," are urged to "put up with" each other—even in what are perceived to be failings—and not to please themselves. This is not a summons to a sort of indifference regarding substantial disagreements. But it is an invitation to refuse to allow those disagreements to sever relationships among those for whom Christ died.

This inclination not to sever relationships may acquire particular importance in our contemporary political and social context. The rise of social media complicates this injunction. More and more, we tend to "follow" people who agree with us and to have fewer online contacts with those who disagree with us. And even those contacts with those with whom we disagree tend to be only negative or even hostile in character, weakening relationships and emphasizing differences rather than commonalities.

Given these social tendencies, it seems to me that Christians are invited to a different social strategy, in the face of political differences. First, Christians are invited to remember that those Christians with whom they disagree are people for whom Christ died, on whom the gospel places enormous value. This in itself suggests different sorts of interactions where the value of such persons rises to a greater prominence. Second, rather than simply voicing disagreements, Christians are invited to discover common ground with those with whom they disagree. This "common ground" begins, of course, with a shared faith in Jesus as the Messiah. But it does not end there. Christians are invited not only to identify their shared values but also to talk about why they may order those values differently, and how such different orderings may arise from distinctive elements within their own experience.

This, of course, is no assurance that agreement will come quickly. If the letters of Paul are at all relevant, agreement may be hard to come by, and may often take a long time. But this is an invitation to the relativizing of differences in light of shared deeper commitments, and a willingness to listen carefully to those with whom we disagree, acknowledging our shared humanity or our common life in Christ, or both. And that, in itself, is an enormously important contribution to the wider political debate in America.

Discussion Questions

- How have you experienced political conflict in your life?
- What do you make of the way this chapter interprets Matthew 22:15–22, particularly Jesus's answer to the question? Should followers of Jesus pay taxes?
- How should Christians deal with their disagreements over the role of government, as this chapter explores the problem?
- How has social media affected the issues addressed in this chapter?
- What do you make of the social strategy at the end of this chapter? Is it helpful or not?

For Further Exploration

DeYoung, John. "Social Concerns." Pages 111–29 in *Piety and Patriotism: 1776–1976*, edited by James W. Van Hoeven. Grand Rapids: Eerdmans, 1976.

Granberg-Michaelson, Wesley. *Future Faith: Ten Challenges Reshaping Christianity in the 21st Century*. Minneapolis: Fortress, 2018.

Labberton, Mark, ed. *Still Evangelical? Insiders Reconsider Political, Social, and Theological Meaning*. Downers Grove, IL: InterVarsity, 2018.

Longman, Tremper, III. *The Bible and the Ballot: Using Scripture for Political Decisions*. Grand Rapids: Eerdmans, 2020.

5 ‖ Sexuality

Doesn't Christianity have a repressive sexual ethic?

‖ Romans 1:18–32

Let's be clear from the get-go: Christianity does not have a great track record in the field of sexual ethics. In a number of ways, in a variety of historical contexts, the way Christians think about sexual ethics has shifted in significant ways, reflecting a difficulty for Christians throughout the history of the faith to arrive at clear teaching. For example, in the earliest years of the Christian tradition, theologians like Augustine and Ambrose seem to take a very dim view of sexuality, even within marriage. Ambrose, for example, believed that the *only* time that even married couples should have sex was when they were intending to make babies. Thus, he insisted, in his commentary on the Gospel of Luke, that it was immoral for a husband and wife to have sex while the wife is pregnant, since such an act cannot be procreative. Later ethical reflection softened this stance, and the Catholic Church now only insists that sex must be "open to procreation." In taking such a position, the Catholic Church has rejected same-sex relationships but apparently sees no problem marrying a heterosexual couple where the woman has had a hysterectomy, since such a couple is at least "open to procreation" (whatever that may mean concretely).

But it is not only such positions on procreation that create problems for the church. In my growing-up years, the crucial issue among Christians in my town was divorce and remarriage. Many divorced and remarried couples were placed under discipline and were unable to partake of communion again unless they divorced their second spouse. Talk about mixed messages regarding divorce!

It's not surprising, then, that many people in our culture today are questioning whether sex and marriage even belong together. More and more young people are putting off marriage, or avoiding it altogether, while having few scruples about living together in sexual relationships, particularly since birth control has severed the long-standing, close linkage between sex and childbearing. That has been true, regardless of the controversy stirred up by the Supreme Court in its *Obergefell* decision in 2015 legalizing same-sex marriage throughout the country—a decision that has only exacerbated conflicts and controversy throughout the country. So the question with which this chapter begins is a lively one!

From a Christian perspective, however, there is a core issue at stake in the way people need to think about sexuality. It has to do with the role of *desire*. Here is one of those points where Christian faith seeks to adopt a substantially different view from that found in the dominant culture today. In our contemporary culture, corporations spend billions of dollars seeking to persuade all of us that we have an obligation—perhaps even a moral obligation—to pursue whatever we desire. (And of course, these same corporations spend billions of dollars seeking to create in us desires for their products!)

But Christians take a different approach. One of the core Christian convictions is that desire, by itself, is not a sufficient warrant for any behavior. The reason, of course, is that desire is essentially focused on oneself, whereas Christian love calls us to focus not on what we want but on what is best for others and for all. When we focus only on our own desires, we act selfishly, rather than in love.

The former archbishop of Canterbury Rowan Williams produced in 1989 a fascinating analysis of desire in his lecture entitled "The Body's Grace" (available on the Internet). In it he notes that what we want the most is not simply to be gratified but to *be desired*. This requires that we pay attention not primarily to our own desires but to the desires of the person we long for. This movement from the self to the other lies at the heart of a Christian ethic of love. To be gratified ourselves, we have to think of someone else, and not just ourselves. *Eros*, meaning self-oriented (often sexually oriented) desire, must give way to *agapē*, self-giving love.

This is the core rationale behind the Bible's critique of lust. We see this clearly in Colossians 3:5, in which "fornication" (the Bible's core word for sexual immorality) is followed by references to "passion, evil desire, and greed (which is idolatry)." Lust ends up expressing itself as greed, and greed is idolatrous in an important sense: it places the person at the center of the universe, rather than God.

We see the same pattern at work in a text drawn from the first chapter of Romans, a text commonly cited in the debates over same-sex relationships and marriage: Romans 1:18–32.

> [18] For the wrath of God is revealed from heaven against all ungodliness and wickedness of those who by their wickedness suppress the truth. [19] For what can be

known about God is plain to them, because God has shown it to them. [20] Ever since the creation of the world his eternal power and divine nature, invisible though they are, have been understood and seen through the things he has made. So they are without excuse; [21] for though they knew God, they did not honor him as God or give thanks to him, but they became futile in their thinking, and their senseless minds were darkened. [22] Claiming to be wise, they became fools; [23] and they exchanged the glory of the immortal God for images resembling a mortal human being or birds or four-footed animals or reptiles.

[24] Therefore God gave them up in the lusts of their hearts to impurity, to the degrading of their bodies among themselves, [25] because they exchanged the truth about God for a lie and worshiped and served the creature rather than the Creator, who is blessed forever! Amen.

[26] For this reason God gave them up to degrading passions. Their women exchanged natural intercourse for unnatural, [27] and in the same way also the men, giving up natural intercourse with women, were consumed with passion for one another. Men committed shameless acts with men and received in their own persons the due penalty for their error.

[28] And since they did not see fit to acknowledge God, God gave them up to a debased mind and to things that should not be done. [29] They were filled with every kind of wickedness, evil, covetousness, malice. Full of envy, murder, strife, deceit, craftiness, they are gossips, [30] slanderers, God-haters, insolent, haughty, boastful, inventors of evil, rebellious toward parents,

³¹ foolish, faithless, heartless, ruthless. ³² They know God's decree, that those who practice such things deserve to die—yet they not only do them but even applaud others who practice them.

The central problem with which this text begins is the tendency of people to "suppress the truth" about God. Paul argues that this truth, consisting of God's "eternal power and divine nature" (v. 20), is evident in the creation, but that human beings have a deeply implanted impulse to ignore this truth and to refuse to honor God. As a result, in verse 26 Paul declares that God "gave them up to degrading passions." What follows is a listing of sexual misconduct, focusing (for the most part) on same-sex behavior. There is some debate about whether the behavior of women reported in verse 26b ("Their women exchanged natural intercourse for unnatural") is same-sex behavior or simply nonreproductive sexual behavior such as oral or anal sex. But verse 27 is unambiguous in describing men as being "consumed with passion for one another."

This brings us to a crucial issue in interpreting Romans 1. Those who adopt a traditionalist sexual ethic emphasize that the abandonment of creation entails the abandonment of the roles of male and female established in the creation. However, that does not, in itself, explain why Paul describes this behavior as "consumed with passion." Yet if one examines ancient sources, one finds a fairly simple explanation for why same-sex behavior was regarded in the ancient world as "consumed with passion." In the ancient world, we don't see anything like the modern notion of sexual orientation. In particular, we don't see any descriptions of men who are attracted only to other men. Instead, we find a different rationale for same-sex behavior. It is described in ancient texts as the result of insatiable passion, a passion that is not content with more "normal" heterosexual gratification, but which is driven by a thirst for the exotic. (For more detailed discussion, see the chapter on lust and desire in my book *Bible, Gender, Sexuality*, listed in "For Further Exploration.")

We see this, for example, in the words of the Roman orator Dio Chrysostom, writing shortly before the time Paul wrote Romans.

> The man whose appetite is insatiate in such things, when he finds there is no scarcity, no resistance, in this field, will have contempt for the easy conquest and scorn for a woman's love, as a thing too readily given— in fact, too utterly feminine—and will turn his assault against the male quarters, eager to befoul the youth who will very soon be magistrates and judges and generals, believing that in them he will find a kind of pleasure difficult and hard to procure. His state is like that of men who are addicted to drinking and wine-bibbing, who after long and steady drinking of unmixed wine, often lose their taste for it and create an artificial thirst by the stimulus of sweating, salted foods, and condiments. (Dio Chrysostom, *Venator* 151–152)

Now, I think we can all agree that sexual behavior that is driven simply by passion and a thirst for the exotic is deeply problematic. Such behavior is self-centered, oblivious to the damage that may be caused to a sexual partner, or to the needs and desires of a sexual partner. Even in our modern, more permissive context, it would not be hard to find many people who agree with this reason for rejecting such behavior. But the crucial question is this: Do Paul's assumptions about the origin of same-sex behavior apply to all LGBTQ people today? Is same-sex behavior always driven by a thirst for the exotic that is uncontent with heterosexual gratification? I think most people would say the answer to that question is no. Where same-sex behavior today is driven by this self-centered thirst for the exotic, there Paul's critique in Romans 1 may apply. But where there is faithfulness and commitment, and such relationships are marked by abiding loyalty, it is hard to see the self-serving, "consumed with passion" description that Paul speaks about as relevant.

So we come to a dividing of the ways with respect to a Christian sexual ethic. For centuries, there has been a fairly consistent emphasis on what we might call an "objective" sexual ethic. By this view, anything that happens sexually between a man and a woman in the covenant of marriage is acceptable, and anything that happens sexually outside of that context is unacceptable. This is the ethic that many more secularly oriented people today regard as "repressive." It is viewed as repressive for two reasons. On the one hand, it fails to offer any qualitative perspective on what counts for good sex within marriage; it is only concerned with external boundaries, not internal goals. On the other hand, it fails to offer any reason, other than simply stating "that's the rule," that sex should be reserved for marriage alone. This shape of a "boundary ethic" is simply inadequate to help people to develop a full-blown ethical framework.

By contrast, I believe there is a "centered ethic" that shapes Christianity's view of the proper place of sexuality. It focuses upon the link between sex and the lifelong bonding implicit in kinship. At its heart, it affirms that people should not say with their bodies, by uniting sexually, what they are unwilling or unable to say with the rest of their lives, by living out a lifelong kinship bond.

Note that this position does assume a "boundary": sexual union and the formation of a lifelong kinship bond are seen as two sides of the same coin. Therefore, any form of promiscuity that is driven simply by personal desire is disallowed. Sex is reserved for the covenant of marriage, the formation of a relationship of lifelong kinship.

However, this view of sex focuses not on the male-female nature of the sexual bond (even though that may be applicable in the clear majority of instances), but rather on the relationship between sex and kinship, and the bonding that is integral to the sexual relationship. Kinship, of course, is not gender-specific. You are just as much kin to your brothers as to your sisters. So by focusing on the link between sex and kinship, we find a way to affirm the Bible's lofty treatment of the marriage bond as the source of kinship, but we also find more focus, and more flexibility. We establish a central purpose for our sexuality—the establishment of lifelong bonds of love. But we also create space for different forms of bonding than one finds in traditional marriage, including same-sex bonds that are marked by lifelong covenant love.

So, does Christianity have a repressive sexual ethic? Sadly, at many points in the history of the Christian faith, the answer to this question has been yes. But in this chapter, I have tried to argue that the core of a Christian sexual ethic, particularly when it is construed not so much as a "bounded" ethic but as a "centered" one, has the potential of speaking much more helpfully to decisions we face about sexual ethics today. This sort of ethic invites us to consider, in a variety of circumstances, what we are "saying" with our bodies, and whether that coheres with what we are saying with the rest of our lives. It is difficult to see how this sort of question is "repressive." It simply invites us to look at our lives and to move toward greater consistency and coherence.

Discussion Questions

- This chapter talks about ambivalences in the Christian tradition over sexual ethics. How serious a problem is this, in your circles?
- How significantly has the advent of birth control changed the discussion about sexual ethics for Christians?
- What do you make of this chapter's interpretation of Romans 1:18–32?
- What do you make of this chapter's distinction between a "bounded" set and a "centered" set with respect to sexual ethics? How helpful is this?

For Further Exploration

Brownson, James V. *Bible, Gender, Sexuality: Reframing the Church's Debate on Same-Sex Relationships*. Grand Rapids: Eerdmans, 2013.

Gary, Sally. *Affirming: A Memoir of Faith, Sexuality, and Staying in the Church*. Grand Rapids: Eerdmans, 2020.

Keen, Karen R. *Scripture, Ethics, and the Possibility of Same-Sex Relationships*. Grand Rapids: Eerdmans, 2018.

6 ∥ Other Religions

***What makes Jesus more important
than Muhammad, Buddha, or
other religious leaders?***

∥ *John 1:1–18*

In this chapter, we will not focus on detailed claims to the truth found in various religions such as Islam, Hinduism, or Buddhism. Instead, our focus will fall on Christian claims about the relative significance of Jesus, particularly as these claims engage other religious perspectives. The emphasis will fall on the particular claim that some Christians make in relation to other religions, that Christianity is a superior religion. Certainly, the passage we are looking at in this chapter (John 1:1–18) appears at first glance to make such claims.

> [1] In the beginning was the Word, and the Word was with God, and the Word was God. [2] He was in the beginning with God. [3] All things came into being through him, and without him not one thing came into being. What has come into being [4] in him was life, and the life was the light of all people. [5] The light shines in darkness, and the darkness did not overcome it.
> [6] There was a man sent from God, whose name was John. [7] He came as a witness to testify to the light, so

that all might believe through him. [8] He himself was not the light, but he came to testify to the light. [9] The true light, which enlightens everyone, was coming into the world.

[10] He was in the world, and the world came into being through him; yet the world did not know him. [11] He came to what was his own, and his own people did not accept him. [12] But to all who received him, who believed in his name, he gave power to become children of God, [13] who were born, not of blood or of the will of the flesh or of the will of man, but of God.

[14] And the Word became flesh and lived among us, and we have seen his glory, the glory as of a father's only son, full of grace and truth. [15] (John testified to him and cried out, "This was he of whom I said, 'He who comes after me ranks ahead of me because he was before me.'") [16] From his fullness we have all received, grace upon grace. [17] The law indeed was given through Moses; grace and truth came through Jesus Christ. [18] No one has ever seen God. It is God the only Son, who is close to the Father's heart, who has made him known.

In the very first verse, Jesus's preexistence as "the Word" is portrayed, along with his agency in the creation of the world. The final verse of our text summarizes the Christian claim: "No one has ever seen God. It is God the only Son, who is close to the Father's heart, who has made him known."

This issue is, of course, complicated by the link between Western Christianity and Western imperialism.

The same countries that claimed to be following Jesus also dominated and controlled much of the world in the period after the Enlightenment. Hence the claim for the ultimacy of God's revelation in Jesus can be seen as a claim for the ultimacy of the governments that made (or, in some cases, continue to make) this claim, along with the subordination of all competing claims. It is important to state clearly, from the beginning, that this is not an adequate basis for resolving such disputes, and this chapter seeks explicitly to avoid any linkage with such forms of argument. Western Christianity comes quite a bit later than the New Testament, and one needs to be careful not to read the New Testament as if it were an expression of later Christian issues, as important as those later issues may be.

One common strategy to counter these problems, particularly among those of a more liberal persuasion, is to use the analogy of paths leading up a mountain. There are many such paths, the saying goes, but they all lead to the same peak of the mountain. In the same way, there are many different religions, but they are all headed in the same ultimate direction. But this presupposes that we have a vantage point from which we can see the mountain, and that we can see that all the paths lead to the same point at the top. Such a conclusion is not immediately evident from an examination of the religions themselves; they differ materially on some points that appear to be substantial. This includes questions such as who is God and what is God like? There are also problems with what faithful obedience looks like.

Indeed, a range of distinctly Christian themes seems problematic from such a more inclusive perspective.

We are left with some uncertainty about how to interpret Christian claims about the uniqueness of Jesus. This "climbing the mountain" image presupposes, instead, that rationalism of one sort or another is what tells us that the various religions are moving ultimately in the same direction. It presumes a more "objective" and thus distant perspective from which such claims may be justified.

This somewhat rationalistic perspective is not what this chapter will pursue. But in the absence of this sort of frame, we do face a series of mounting complexities when thinking about the challenge that world religions pose to each other. The Enlightenment movement toward rationalization and modernization led many people to assume that all religions would eventually die out, but that has not happened. Yet the modern world has impacted religion in major ways and in subtle ways. The rise of immigration and the emergence of the Internet have brought people from various religions into deeper contact with each other, further complexifying religious identity and religious practice. At the same time, the increasing opportunities, in a variety of ways, for people around the world to stay in touch with others of a similar mind-set have provided support for diversity, even in the midst of cross-cultural encounters. This pattern has provided grounds for resistance to otherwise harmonizing tendencies in many cultural contexts. Moreover, the rise of individualism around the world renders these issues still more complex, as religions morph in sometimes surprising ways, incorporating individualism in new ways into their belief structures.

All these social phenomena affect in significant ways the nature and character of the relations between different religions in the world today, and each of them could easily absorb our attention in this chapter. But our focus here is somewhat different: What does Christianity itself say and assume about other religions? It may be useful, in exploring this topic, to start with verse 4 of our text: "in him [i.e., in the Word, which is Jesus] was life, and the life was the light of all people." We see here a clear claim to a final and ultimate revelation, similar to what we find in many other religions as well. In other words, Christianity does not presume that it exists alongside other religions, offering one path among many others to the divine. Instead, it claims, like many other religions, to present the clearest, final, and ultimate path to the divine, even though other religions may disagree about the nature and character of that path. Christians claim that in Christ we see life, and that life is the light of *all* people (v. 4), not merely of those Christians who believe in this form of life.

Yet this claim is also qualified in some very significant ways. The first qualification appears in verse 11: "He came to what was his own, and his own people did not accept him." This claim to a finality of revelation in Christ is not accompanied by a claim to the social superiority of those who might make that claim. One only needs to think of people like Nicodemus, who voices his suspicions about Jesus in John 3, or the family of Jesus in John 7, who (mistakenly) want him to go to Jerusalem, as illustrations of this dynamic. In fact, the Gospel of John devotes quite a bit of attention to the multiple ways in which well-meaning people resisted and opposed God's self-revelation in Christ, and how such folk were loved by God regardless of this behavior.

Thus any claim to linkage between the religious superiority of God's self-revelation in Jesus and the social superiority of followers of Jesus is significantly relativized. This text witnesses to a form of Christian belief that is profoundly self-critical: ultimate revelation is found in Jesus, not in my understanding or conception of Jesus. We see this stated even more clearly in the last verse in our passage, verse 18: "No one has ever seen God. It is God the only Son, who is close to the Father's heart, who has made him known."

This means, ironically, that to affirm the ultimate truth found in Jesus is not necessarily to disparage other sources of wisdom and revelation, even from outside one's own religious framework. If indeed "no one has ever seen God," then no one can claim superiority for their own knowledge or understanding.

This is a radical implication of Christian faith in particular, not necessarily replicated in other religions (though present to some extent in a variety of other religions). The implication is simple and important: to affirm that ultimate truth is found in Jesus is not necessarily to disparage other sources of wisdom and revelation. Nor does such a claim entail an accompanying claim of religious superiority on the part of those who hold it.

We see this concretely and tangibly in the emergence of early Christianity. One of the ways this shows itself is in the approach to language itself. Christianity has never had trouble with being translated into other languages. From the beginning, Jesus spoke Aramaic, but the New Testament documents—including the words of Jesus—were written, not in Aramaic, but in Greek. The New Testament itself was quickly translated into other languages as well. From the beginning, there was nothing sacred about particular linguistic formulations, and other languages helped to shed light on the revelation that was found in Christ.

So Christianity may make claims about the revelation that has come to us in Christ, but this does not translate into a notion of the superiority of the Christian religion or of particular Christian religious practitioners. Rather, Christianity is marked by an eagerness to learn from others who may be different from us, even from practitioners of different religions. So there are indeed claims made by Christianity about the finality of God's self-revelation in Christ, but this does not necessarily translate into religious claims of superiority in relationship to other religions.

Discussion Questions

- What other religions have you encountered, and how does this chapter speak to those encounters?
- How compatible is John 1:1–18 with the claims of other religions?
- This chapter asserts a link between Western Christianity and Western imperialism. How significant a problem is this?
- What do you make of the critique of the "paths up the mountain" image in this chapter? Does this analogy hold in your circles?
- How have more recent changes in immigration and related issues changed this conversation?

For Further Exploration

Bruner, Frederick Dale. *The Gospel of John: A Commentary.*
    Grand Rapids: Eerdmans, 2012. Pages 3–59.
Freedman, David Noel, and Michael J. McClymond, eds. *The
    Rivers of Paradise: Moses, Buddha, Confucius, Jesus,
    and Muhammad as Religious Founders.* Grand Rapids:
    Eerdmans, 2001.
Hill, Graham. *Salt, Light, and a City: Introducing Missional
    Ecclesiology.* Eugene, OR: Wipf & Stock, 2012.
Kärkkäinen, Veli-Matti. *Doing the Work of Comparative The-
    ology: A Primer for Christians.* Grand Rapids: Eerd-
    mans, 2020.
Milbank, John. *Theology and Social Theory: Beyond Secular
    Reason.* Cambridge, MA: Blackwell, 1990.

7 ∦ Failures

Don't the moral failures
of a significant number of
Christian leaders call the whole
of Christianity into question?

∦ *Matthew 23:1–12*

This is not a good time for leaders in Christian churches. The #MeToo and #ChurchToo movements have called attention, particularly on social media, to multiple cases where Christian male leaders have sexually abused female members of their communities. In other contexts, some Christian leaders have been guilty of problematic financial dealings. We hear often, and in great detail, about the moral failings of Christian leaders. Many in our culture regard Christian faith as deeply problematic, as a result of these failings.

In this context, we will be looking at Matthew 23:1–12.

[1] Then Jesus said to the crowds and to his disciples, [2] "The scribes and the Pharisees sit on Moses' seat; [3] therefore, do whatever they teach you and follow it; but do not do as they do, for they do not practice what they teach. [4] They tie up heavy burdens, hard to bear, and lay them on the shoulders of others; but they themselves are unwilling to lift a finger to move them.

⁵ They do all their deeds to be seen by others; for they
make their phylacteries broad and their fringes long.
⁶ They love to have the place of honor at banquets and
the best seats in the synagogues, ⁷ and to be greeted
with respect in the marketplaces, and to have people
call them rabbi. ⁸ But you are not to be called rabbi, for
you have one teacher, and you are all students. ⁹ And
call no one your father on earth, for you have one Father—the one in heaven. ¹⁰ Nor are you to be called
instructors, for you have one instructor, the Messiah.
¹¹ The greatest among you will be your servant. ¹² All
who exalt themselves will be humbled, and all who
humble themselves will be exalted."

The concern over the failings of religious leaders is
not a new thing. In Matthew's Gospel, Jesus devotes an
enormous amount of time to talking about the failures of
leaders, and this text is a classic example. Moreover, this
is not simply a complaint about Jewish leaders (i.e., the
scribes and Pharisees). Verses 8–12 make it clear (by the
use of "you") that the same sorts of problems, temptations, and difficulties afflict leaders in Matthew's church
as well, and by extension, the followers of Jesus today.

But it's not that leadership itself is the problem. Jesus
acknowledges that there are legitimate and appropriate
leadership functions. He points out how the scribes and
Pharisees sit "on Moses' seat." According to Dale Bruner,
"Israel had a tradition that the Lord built Moses a chair on
Sinai, from which the law was handed down from Moses
to Joshua to the elders to prophets and so on down to
the present Bible teachers" (*The Churchbook: Matthew
13–28*, 432). In other words, Matthew's Jesus affirms that

these Jewish leaders are in the position of handing down revelation from God that must be taken seriously. Insofar as they are handing down that revelation, they are to be obeyed. But the problem, of course, is that these leaders, and many later leaders who will follow after them, do not practice what they teach. Their behavior and their teaching don't line up well. (Matthew's Jesus also contests the particular interpretations that these leaders place on various texts at numerous points ["you have heard that it was said"; see, e.g., Matt. 5:21–48], so there is no wholesale endorsement of the teaching of the scribes and Pharisees here.) But one of Matthew's points in our text, particularly when he refers to "Moses' seat," is that there is such a thing as real authority, and that this authority can be rightly delegated to particular persons. We don't see a radical deconstruction of all authority or leadership in Matthew.

However, Matthew's Jesus also recognizes that this authority is difficult and seductive. Those drawn to it are tempted to emphasize the difficult points particularly for outsiders, and to do little to help people to abide by this teaching (see v. 4). They are drawn to the status and honor of the role, rather than to acts of obedience. (Obedience is rarely dramatic or obvious.)

As a result, Matthew's Jesus urges two particular responses in verses 8–12; leaders who follow Jesus are not to claim honorary titles for themselves ("rabbi," "father," or "instructor"). Rather than "exalting themselves," they are to humble themselves, and to take on the posture of a servant of others.

Yet these are not simple instructions to follow. Although Jesus does not mention it explicitly, one can't help but wonder whether contemporary ministerial titles like "Reverend" or "Pastor" might fall under the same sort of critique of titles that we see in our text. Certainly the common way of addressing Catholic priests as "Father" seems echoed here in verse 9. Moreover, although the titles with which I am commonly addressed, "Doctor" and "Professor," aren't explicitly mentioned in this passage, they are not far from the term "instructor," which is included. This is not a passage that the church or its leaders have had a simple and easy time adopting!

But the Gospel of Matthew itself has passages that seem to qualify the radical critique of leadership titles and functions implicit in this text. Consider the Great Commission, found at the very end of the gospel, in Matthew 28:18–20:

> [18] And Jesus came and said to them, "All authority in heaven and on earth has been given to me. [19] Go therefore and make disciples of all nations, baptizing them in the name of the Father and of the Son and of the Holy Spirit, [20] and teaching them to obey everything that I have commanded you. And remember, I am with you always, to the end of the age."

Here the disciples are explicitly charged with a number of tasks, including "teaching them to obey everything that I have commanded you." They may not be called "instructors," but they are clearly assigned teaching tasks. They are to "make disciples" and to baptize these disciples. Once they were merely disciples, but now they are to make others into disciples. They clearly occupy public leadership roles—roles that continued in the church established by them.

So the problem, if we consider Matthew's Gospel as a whole, is not the existence of leaders (that is unavoidable) but rather the seductiveness of the leadership role. In particular, our text highlights a number of temptations:

- Leaders may be tempted to impose burdens on others that they are unwilling to carry themselves (v. 3).
- Not only at times may they fail to do what they teach, but they may be tempted to show little interest in helping people who struggle with obedience, or find it burdensome to help them (v. 4).
- They may often be more deeply motivated by public acclaim than by actually leading people in the right direction (v. 5).
- This core motivation may manifest itself in specific sorts of public behaviors and titles that they find particularly attractive (vv. 6–7).
- Thus, our text calls for alternatives that tilt against these problematic temptations and motivations:
  - Leaders are to avoid honorific titles, particularly those that obscure core beliefs, focusing instead on divine presence and action (vv. 8–10). This divine presence radically relativizes the significance of leaders and refocuses their role and function.
  - Hence, the focus of leadership falls not on status and honor but on humility and service (v. 11).

- And in fact, all leaders who pursue their own status can expect to be "humbled" in the final judgment, and those who humble themselves will be exalted (v. 12).

Unfortunately, these problems with leaders did not disappear with the time of Jesus. In fact, the focal question for this chapter suggests that there are still serious problems with Christian leaders today. So, why do so many Christian leaders have such a hard time following the one whom they proclaim as Teacher and Lord? Why do we see the same sorts of problems with leadership in the church today that Jesus spoke about even before the church came into existence?

Some of this, no doubt, is due to the nature of leadership in almost any context, particularly religious leadership. Religious communities expect leaders to articulate the core values that differentiate those communities from the larger public. And that expectation brings an implicit and powerful temptation to hypocrisy in both leaders and followers, particularly when religious communities have lost sight of a deeper and more transformative vision that may distinguish them from the larger public.

Moreover, leadership roles tend to attract certain types of personalities, who may be more vulnerable to the difficulties addressed in our text in Matthew 23. Contemporary psychologists often refer to this type of personality disorder as "narcissistic." If you Google the phrase "narcissistic leadership," you will find lots of contemporary discussion of this phenomenon, particularly among religious leaders. In fact, 85 percent of all Americans don't want to get up in front of other people and talk, but ministerial leadership sees this as a central task. Clearly, ministers are not typical in their psychological profile.

So there are powerful forces, both in leaders themselves and in the communities and contexts in which they serve, that tend to reinforce these more problematic expressions of leadership. But our text suggests both that these problems were not unknown in the ancient world and that there are forces within Christianity that move leadership into a more productive direction. The first of these more productive forces is the life and example of Jesus himself, who models self-giving service and gives up his life for the sake of those he loves. Leaders are expected to do likewise. The second one identified in the text is the doctrine of radical divine transcendence. Because God is God, and we are not, all Christian leadership must point beyond itself to the one to whom all allegiance is finally due. There is only one parent from whom we draw our life, who is God. A focus on divine transcendence reduces the significance of human leaders. And finally, because Jesus is the Messiah, leaders must always point beyond themselves to the messianic movement of which the church is a part, and from which it draws its identity. These truths are continually drawing the church beyond a focus on its leaders to more fundamental realities.

But human beings always do this imperfectly. This was true in the time of Jesus. It was true for Matthew and the churches to whom he was writing. It continues to be true for the church today. It is precisely the deep and wide-ranging claims made by the church that often entice more neurotic types to seek leadership within the church. These same claims may tempt the church to magnify in unhealthy ways the differences between itself and the larger communities surrounding it, undermining compassion and sacrificial service. These temptations may be particularly evident in the lives of the church's leaders.

The answer, however, does not lie in abandoning those claims to divine presence and action. The answer is found in returning, over and over, to the words of Jesus, and in allowing these words to invite us into a deeper reality—the reality of self-giving and sacrificial service to others. We need leaders who equip the church to hold onto this focus and to live out this life, no matter what may come their way. The church will continue to hear the voice of Jesus calling us to this life, even from outside the walls of the church and its established leadership. For in many cases, this is the only place where this sort of voice can originate, and from which it can speak with life and integrity.

So, yes, the moral failure of a significant number of Christian leaders is a serious problem. But it does not call the Christian faith into question in any fundamental way. As long as the church proclaims and follows after Jesus, it embraces a deeper and wider vision that calls us to a different form of leadership, and it continually invites even leaders to follow in the path of humble service.

Discussion Questions

- Where and how, if at all, have you experienced the moral failure of Christian leaders?
- This chapter suggests that a major source of the problem is leaders acting in their perceived self-interest rather than for the common good. Is this a problem in your circles? Examples?

- Are modern titles for Christian leaders problematic in the way discussed in this chapter? Why or why not?
- Is this chapter realistic in its expectation of Christian leaders? Why or why not?
- Do you agree with the claim at the end of this chapter, that the moral failure of some Christian leaders does not reflect on Christian faith as a whole? Why or why not?

For Further Exploration

Bruner, Frederick Dale. *Matthew: A Commentary.* Vol. 2, *The Churchbook: Matthew 13–28.* Revised and expanded ed. Grand Rapids: Eerdmans, 2004. Pages 428–42.

Janssen, Allan J. *Kingdom, Office, and Church: A Study of A. A. van Ruler's Doctrine of Ecclesiastical Office.* Grand Rapids: Eerdmans, 2006.

Munroe, Myles. *The Power of Character in Leadership: How Values, Morals, Ethics, and Principles Affect Leaders.* New Kensington, PA: Whitaker House, 2014.

8 ∥ Spirituality

*If I'm "spiritual but not religious,"
meaning that I care about spiritual
issues, why should I have time or
energy for religious practices or
communities?*

∥ Romans 12:3–5

It is an increasingly common disposition among young people: they care about Christianity, or at least about faith-related issues in general, but they have little or no interest in the church. They are not interested in participating, with other believers, in a shared faith. There may be any number of reasons why. It may be that the person rejects specific practices he or she sees as common in many churches. It may be that he or she embraces a highly individualistic form of belief that leaves no room for *any* sorts of shared practices. Or it may be that religious practices, even of an individualistic sort, bear no relationship to the form of spiritual life to which the person is drawn.

It may be helpful to look at a particular section of Romans 12 as we seek to address these concerns. I am thinking particularly of Romans 12:3–5.

³ For by the grace given to me I say to everyone among you not to think of yourself more highly than you ought

to think, but to think with sober judgment, each according to the measure of faith that God has assigned. ⁴ For as in one body we have many members, and not all the members have the same function, ⁵ so we, who are many, are one body in Christ, and individually we are members one of another.

The first problem I want to talk about, which this passage addresses, is *individualism*. Individualism is a peculiarly modern problem in the Western world. Many corporations spend billions of dollars every year trying to persuade us that we are primarily individuals, driven by our own thoughts and desires. They spend this money, of course, because their advertising has a profound effect on what we think and desire. So it is to their advantage to persuade us that our thoughts and desires originate only in ourselves, and that this individualistic self lies at the core of our being. When we believe this, we act as they would like us to act, and they make a profit. So the first irony is that when we embrace individualism, we are in fact embracing a perspective that enables profits to increase in the contemporary corporate world.

Another problem with individualism is that it violates, at a profound level, the meaning of biblical texts like the one quoted above. Think of the core image of the body in this passage. Paul begins by asserting, "For as in one body we have many members." It is easy for us to misread what he means by "members." We tend to think the word refers to people who are part of some organization. Ironically, this is in large part due to the effectiveness of Paul's language in this passage. But "members" originally meant, in an ancient context, "body parts." Paul's whole point in this passage is that different parts of the body have different functions but are all part of the same body. So the eye does something no other body part can do: it processes the light that comes to the body and enables the body to see. No other body part can do this. Yet the eyes can't do anything with the information they receive; they must rely on other parts of the body for the effective processing of that information, as well as any appropriate action on that information.

What this means is that, when we turn to "the body" as an image for social groups, we need each other, particularly in diverse ways, to get things done. This stands in dramatic contrast to an individualism that claims we need no one at all and can do everything we need to do by ourselves. Our believing in individualism may help corporations sell us more of their goods and services, but it doesn't help us to function more effectively as the body of Christ. It at least runs the risk of obscuring the ways in which we need each other.

But all this is only a prelude to the central conflict of our focus question: What is the difference between being "spiritual" and being "religious"? For many people, this is a contrast between the material world and some other, "spiritual" world. At stake here is the implicit contrast between matters of the "spirit" and matters of the material world. The assumption is that matters of the spirit have no connection to matters of the material world.

We see this contrast already in writers such as Plato. In the "Allegory of the Cave," part of his *Republic*, he suggests that what we perceive as the "material world" is really just an image, within a cave, of objects that are really outside the cave but casting shadows into the cave. Interestingly, Merriam-Webster's dictionary picks up this meaning and lists as a synonym of "spiritual" in its first definition the word "incorporeal." So, when someone contrasts "spiritual" with "religious," he or she may well be implying that, although "religious" refers to the corporeal world, "spiritual" does not.

This means that, when "spiritual" is contrasted with "religious," "spiritual" persons don't need to worry about material things like attending meetings, or participating in a group, in order to express their "spiritual" nature. Rather, this is a purely personal matter (in that sense, "spiritual"), quite divorced from the material world.

Paul, by contrast, insists, in verse 5, that "we, who are many, are one body in Christ, and individually we are members one of another." Now, I suppose it is possible, at least in a preliminary sense, to consider the body of Christ in a completely nonmaterial way, as a "spiritual" reality, which people partake of whether or not that participation has any material expression in their lives. But this perspective minimizes the significance of the physicality of the body of Christ. The entire creedal tradition of the church insists that Jesus is not only a spiritual being but also a physical being: born of a woman, crucified, suffered, died, and was physically raised from the dead. None of this makes sense if the body of Christ is not physical and material.

But being "spiritual" is contrasted with being "religious," so we need to explore the term "religious" as well. The quote from Romans 12 may not speak to this directly, but the issue is certainly one the New Testament addresses frequently. Many of Jesus's conflicts with the scribes and Pharisees boil down to differing conceptions of what it means to be "religious." Indeed, for the scribes and Pharisees, "religion" means careful observance of the

Torah (according to their interpretation of key texts), as well as a variety of public acts, including public prayer, temple worship, etc. In fact, much of the conflict between Jesus and the scribes and Pharisees centers around different understandings of what it means to be "religious" in the first place.

Here is where the "spiritual but not religious" language ironically captures something important about the teaching of Jesus. Jesus consistently placed the emphasis on *motives* rather than *behavior*, and thus downplayed "religious" observances that lacked a *spiritual* component, particularly in terms of motivation. One thinks of his purging of the merchants in the temple in Matthew 21:12–17 (cf. Mark 11:15–19; Luke 19:45–48; John 2:13–25). Here we see how the profit motives of the sellers in the temple conflicted with religious observance, and how the religious practices of the day undermined the capacity of the average person to worship in the temple.

But this is not a separation of "spiritual" and "religious," and it is not a *rejection* of religious practices (though the scribes and Pharisees may well have looked at Jesus through this lens). Rather, it is an attempt to reunite the spiritual and religious dimensions of life at a much deeper level, in terms of actual practices.

So, if the expression "spiritual but not religious" reflects a rejection of the religious in favor of a nonmaterial "spiritual" understanding, it must be called into question. But if "spiritual but not religious" is in fact calling for a more deeply spiritual expression of religion, rather than a focus on merely external behaviors, then it finds kinship with the teaching of Jesus himself. But this entails not a rejection of religion but its transformation.

Discussion Questions

- Describe instances of "spiritual but not religious" attitudes or behavior from your own experience.
- How serious is the problem of *individualism* addressed by this chapter?
- Does "spiritual" mean "incorporeal" in your circles? What impact does this have on the discussion?
- What is a healthy integration of spirituality and religious practice? What does it look like?

For Further Exploration

Hurtado, Larry W. *Lord Jesus Christ: Devotion to Jesus in Earliest Christianity*. Grand Rapids: Eerdmans, 2003.

Schneiders, Sandra M. "Spirituality." In *The New Interpreter's Dictionary of the Bible*, vol. 5. Nashville: Abingdon, 2009.

9 ∥ *Fruitfulness*

> *Why do so many Christians avoid*
> *living a loving and productive*
> *Christian life that honors God?*
>
> ∥ *1 Peter 2:1–3, 9–10*

There are a number of significant issues implicit in this question. We see problems like an excessive emphasis in many Christian circles on grace and the avoidance of any sort of fruitfulness or productivity. In these contexts, fruitfulness is equated with legalism and is to be avoided at all costs. What is at stake is a doctrine of grace.

This is no small matter! Christianity is, above all else, a religion that invites people to embrace a life of grace. Generosity, kindness, acceptance—these are all critical to being a Christian in the first place, and Christians whose lives do not reflect these realities are not living by grace, and therefore are failing to honor God and to reflect the divine disposition toward the world in their lives, regardless of how much they may talk about grace. Grace is something, at its core, that is *lived*, not just talked about. This is the first issue that is implicit in this question.

But this failure to live by grace is closely related to another issue: the problem of avoidance as a general theme in many Christian circles. Far too many Christians define themselves more by what they avoid than by what they affirm. Within this problematic perspective, being a Christian is defined, at its core, in terms of the avoidance of specific behaviors that stand in opposition to a life of grace. Avoidance and lack of fruitfulness are thus closely related issues. One tends to go hand in hand with the other.

We see related issues quite clearly in the way the death of Jesus is interpreted in church history. I discovered this when I began to translate martyr stories from other languages, as part of my PhD program long ago. I discovered that, prior to the conversion of Constantine in the fourth century, Christianity was defined primarily as a form of resistance to the Roman Empire. That resistance was understood, in these early centuries, to be the central meaning of the death of Jesus. Rome used crucifixion as a powerful means to terrorize the most potentially dangerous populations into submission. Jesus's crucifixion by the Roman Empire was clearly understood to be an expression of this general policy. Consequently, to be understood as a follower of Jesus clearly meant that, even if you were not explicitly opposed to Rome, at least you did not respect Rome in the way most Roman citizens did.

Consequently, most of the early stories coming out of Christian faith were in fact martyr stories, stories of the death of believers at the hands of the Roman Empire. One need only look at the writings of early church fathers like Justin Martyr or Ignatius or Polycarp to see this very clearly. A simple Internet search of any of these names will bring up the texts, along with core realities: Jesus died to reconcile us to God, to be sure, but Jesus did this by showing us the path to living with the divine, and that path (at least in the Roman Empire) was also the road to martyrdom. Just as Jesus was crucified by the Roman Empire, so followers of Jesus should accept the same fate, at least as a significant possibility. This was the concrete form taken by a fruitful life as Christianity began.

This stands in dramatic contrast to the teaching of the church after the conversion of Constantine. The focus remains on the death of Jesus, but the story of his death and its significance is recounted quite differently. Rather than being a story about fruitfulness amidst resistance to the Roman Empire, it becomes a story of how we are reconciled to God: Jesus bears the punishment we deserved on the cross, so that we could be free. In all this, Paul's letter to the Romans acquires particular significance since Paul, already in this letter written early in Christian history, had good reason to downplay resistance to the Roman Empire and to emphasize the reconciliatory power of the death of Jesus, since he was writing a letter to Christians who resided at the center of the empire, in Rome itself! He had no desire to create additional trouble for Christians who already stood under suspicion in Rome. The Roman emperor Claudius had already expelled the Jews from Rome prior to the writing of this letter. The expulsion from Rome is mentioned in Acts 18:2, where Paul meets Aquila, who the text tells us was expelled from Italy because Emperor Claudius ordered all Jews to leave Rome.

So the martyrdom of Jesus as an expression of resistance to Rome in earlier years turned into the means by which we are reconciled to God in this later period, after the conversion of Constantine, as the primary interpretation of the meaning of the death of Jesus. Resistance and reconciliation are not mutually exclusive options of course, but the emphasis shifts noticeably, particularly concerning the authority being addressed: we see a movement in much of Christian literature from a focus on Rome to a focus on reconciliation with God. Along with this shift in focus comes a shift away from the importance of what *we* do (in resisting the attractiveness of the Roman Empire) to what *God* does for us (in reconciling us to God despite our sinfulness). In this shift, what we do becomes much more devoid of significance. Christianity is no longer about what we do but rather about what God does for us in Christ. The emphasis shifts from obedience to trusting in grace. This becomes particularly evident in the shift away from martyr stories as a focus.

This concern with human behavior is clearly evident in the initial verses from our text for this chapter. First Peter 2:1–3 expresses this focus on following the crucified one:

> [1] Rid yourselves, therefore, of all malice, and all guile, insincerity, envy, and all slander. [2] Like newborn infants, long for the pure, spiritual milk, so that by it you may grow into salvation— [3] if indeed you have tasted that the Lord is good.

This passage presupposes, of course, a framework of grace. Note how verse 3 focuses on the goodness of the Lord. But the appropriate response, listed in the opening verse, is to "rid yourselves, therefore, of all malice and all guile, insincerity, envy, and all slander." This is what it means to "grow into salvation" in verse 2. In other words, behav-

ioral change in the believer is not so much the response
to salvation as it is the expression of salvation. It is what
maturity looks like, when one leaves childhood behind.

Why do so many contemporary Christians avoid this? It
is because they fear that Christianity will become a religion
of works, losing its emphasis on the grace of God, given to
us despite our unworthiness. The irony, of course, is that in
so doing they stop treating other people with graciousness
and stop giving away their own lives, calling into question
the very reality to which they hope to bear witness.

This is the problem that is the focus of this chapter.
And it becomes particularly evident in the conclusion to
the 1 Peter 2 passage.

> [9] But you are a chosen race, a royal priesthood, a holy
> nation, God's own people, in order that you may pro-
> claim the mighty acts of him who called you out of
> darkness into his marvelous light.
>
> > [10] Once you were not a people,
> >   but now you are God's people;
> > once you had not received mercy,
> >   but now you have received mercy.

That is to say, receiving mercy is what constitutes
Christians as a people, *and* what distinguishes them from
others. This is what makes them "a chosen people, a royal
priesthood, a holy nation." But this also affects behavior,
comprehensively, and often deeply. It is not only whether
we have received grace but also whether our lives have
been changed to reflect this reality in everyday life. It is

important to keep both of these perspectives in mind. We need to be concerned not only with what constitutes us as a people but also with our behavior, and what distinguishes us from others. This means we must also actively resist all attempts society makes to order our life for us in ways that diminish the significance of our following of Jesus. Grace necessarily changes the way we live.

Discussion Questions

- In your context, is the emphasis more on fruitfulness or on avoidance?
- Is there an excessive emphasis in many Christian circles on grace *and* the avoidance of fruitfulness? What about your circles?
- What do you make of the changes in approach to the death of Jesus narrated in this chapter? Is this a problem in your circles?
- What do you make of 1 Peter 2:1–3, 9–10 as this chapter interprets them? Is this part of the solution to this problem?
- What would you say is the relationship between grace and obedience?

For Further Exploration

Liftin, Bryan M. *Early Christian Martyr Stories: An Evangelical Introduction with New Translations*. Grand Rapids: Baker Academic, 2014.

Michaels, J. Ramsey. *1 Peter*. Word Biblical Commentary. Waco, TX: Word, 1988. Pages 82–120.

Pagitt, Doug. *Outdoing Jesus: Seven Ways to Live Out the Promise of "Greater Than."* Grand Rapids: Eerdmans, 2019.

Westerholm, Stephen. "Grace." In *The New Interpreter's Dictionary of the Bible*, vol. 2. Nashville: Abingdon, 2007.

I have been hurt by the church in the past. Why should I bother with it now?

∥ *Hebrews 12:14–29*

The word "church" in this question is ambiguous. While it can refer to all Christians, the reference to "hurt" in the question suggests something more particular. There was a specific set of Christians somewhere who did something that hurt the person who raises this question. But that assumes that another group of Christians would do the same thing or act in the same way. And even if the "hurt" were the result of Christians acting *as Christians*, and not simply on their own behalf, other Christians may disagree with what those Christians did that was hurtful. The question of *why* some Christians acted in a way that was hurtful needs to be explored, but it is unaddressed by the above question.

We need to explore the specific form of hurt involved here. Were the people acting *as Christians*, or were they *failing* to follow Jesus, when they did what was hurtful? If it's the latter, then this is hardly a determinative issue for Christianity as a whole. One might wish to avoid this particular congregation, but the problem says nothing essential about Christians in general. But even if the problem is a more generic one in which the church was attempting to follow Jesus when they hurt the person, there is no unavoidable indication that other Christians would necessarily agree. Let's consider a specific example: the issue of LGBTQ membership in a local church. It may well be that a particular congregation seeks to preserve its Christian identity by refusing to admit an LGBTQ person into full membership in the church. But other Christians would disagree and go out of their way to welcome such a person into full membership, also in the name of Christ. So the fact that *some* Christians hurt someone does not necessarily mean that *all* Christians would do the same thing.

So, it is one thing to assert that some Christians hurt me by attempting to act as Christians. It is quite another to assert that all Christians would take this same approach. That means my conflict may not be with Christianity as a religion but with a particular interpretation of Christian faith put forward by some who are attempting to follow Jesus. In such a context, finding a different gathering of Christians who would not hurt me in the same way is completely understandable, and one way to resolve this dilemma.

But there is another emphasis in Christian faith that moves in a very different direction from hurt and division, particularly in the context of relationships that cannot be avoided. I'm thinking particularly of the focus in many biblical texts upon the dynamics of reconciliation. One thinks of texts such as Romans 5:11, which reads, "But more than that, we even boast in God through our Lord Jesus Christ, through whom we have now received reconciliation." This is echoed in 2 Corinthians 5:18, which reads, "All this is from God, who reconciled us to himself through Christ, and has given us the ministry of reconciliation." Reconciliation assumes, of course, the presence and reality of some form of hurt. However, it also presupposes that the hurt is not the end of that relationship.

This reality lies at the heart of Jesus's command to "love your enemies" (Matt. 5:44; Luke 6:27). Such a command presupposes that people will unavoidably hurt each other, and the result will be animosity, with people even becoming enemies of each other. But according to Jesus, this is not the last word. Rather, believers are to imitate their God, who sends both sun and rain on the just and the unjust. Kindness, rather than justice, marks the last word in ethics. This means, of course, that the assumptions that are implicit in the question that defines this chapter are problematic, since those assumptions are that when people hurt you, you have no further responsibility to engage them at all. However, if we are to love our enemies, this is no longer the same sort of option.

Hence, the command to love your enemies has a theistic focus, but it also implies a relational expression. We are to love our enemies because this is the pattern of the God we worship. But that pattern has concrete implications for our relationships as well. This has significant implications for how we interpret Hebrews 12:24, particularly in its reference to "the sprinkled blood that speaks a better word than the blood of Abel." What is at stake in this reference is the conflict between the first two brothers born to the human race, narrated in Genesis 4. We learn here that Cain killed Abel because his sacrifice was not received in the way that Abel's was. He responds with violence when he does not get his way.

But the portrayal of the death of Jesus, the "sprinkled blood" of our passage from Hebrews 12:14–29, speaks "a better word" than the blood of Abel. Here is the text:

> [14] Pursue peace with everyone, and the holiness without which no one will see the Lord. [15] See to it that no one fails to obtain the grace of God; that no root of bitterness springs up and causes trouble, and through it many become defiled. [16] See to it that no one becomes like Esau, an immoral and godless person, who sold his birthright for a single meal. [17] You know that later, when he wanted to inherit the blessing, he was rejected, for he found no chance to repent, even though he sought the blessing with tears.
>
> [18] You have not come to something that can be touched, a blazing fire, and darkness, and gloom, and a tempest, [19] and the sound of a trumpet, and a voice whose words made the hearers beg that not another word be spoken to them. [20] (For they could not endure the order that was given, "If even an animal touches the mountain, it shall be stoned to death." [21] Indeed, so terrifying was the sight that Moses said, "I tremble with fear.") [22] But you have come to Mount Zion and to the city of the living God, the heavenly Jerusalem, and to innumerable angels in festal gathering, [23] and to the assembly of the firstborn who are enrolled in heaven, and to God the judge of all, and to the spirits of the righteous made perfect, [24] and to Jesus, the mediator of a new covenant, and to the sprinkled blood that speaks a better word than the blood of Abel.
>
> [25] See that you do not refuse the one who is speaking; for if they did not escape when they refused the

one who warned them on earth, how much less will
we escape if we reject the one who warns from heaven!
²⁶ At that time his voice shook the earth; but now he
has promised, "Yet once more I will shake not only the
earth but also the heaven." ²⁷ This phrase, "Yet once
more," indicates the removal of what is shaken—that
is, created things—so that what cannot be shaken may
remain. ²⁸ Therefore, since we are receiving a kingdom
that cannot be shaken, let us give thanks, by which we
offer to God an acceptable worship with reverence and
awe; ²⁹ for indeed our God is a consuming fire.

The blood of Abel (v. 24) narrates a conflict that is
never resolved in the text of Genesis. While Adam and
Eve go on to have other sons who continue the line of
redemption, Cain is marked by God in Genesis 4:15 so
that no one would kill him. But the implication of this
long passage from Hebrews is that the death of Jesus, the
free gift of his life for his enemies, speaks a different and
better word than the death of Abel. We see not simply the
limitation of violence, as in the story of Abel, but rather
the exhaustion of violence in the death of Jesus, and the
start of something dramatically new.

So two basic responses emerge from this passage to
the question of this chapter. The first is simply to differentiate between what particular Christians do and the
teaching of Christian faith itself. This differentiation may
lead some folks to seek another fellowship in some instances. But at a deeper level, Christian faith calls all of us
to love our enemies. This means we don't have the option
of simply writing off those with whom we disagree, but we
need to find creative ways to work at these troubling and

problematic relationships. If Christianity is not expressive of reconciliation, it is not Christianity in the first place.

Discussion Questions

- Have you been hurt by the church? How and when?
- This chapter makes a big deal about the distinction between what *some* Christians say and what Christians say in general. How useful is this distinction in your context?
- What do you make of the "dynamics of reconciliation" in this chapter? Is this helpful?
- What does it look like in your context for people to love their enemies? Is this easy or hard?
- When is separation from other Christians a helpful answer, and when is it a problem?

For Further Exploration

Das, A. Andrew. "Reconciliation." In *The New Interpreter's Dictionary of the Bible*, vol. 4. Nashville: Abingdon, 2009.

Janssen, Allan J., ed. *A Ministry of Reconciliation: Essays in Honor of Gregg Mast*. Grand Rapids: Eerdmans, 2017.

Small, Joseph D. *Flawed Church, Faithful God: A Reformed Ecclesiology for the Real World*. Grand Rapids: Eerdmans, 2018.

11 ∥ Abuse

Large numbers of religious leaders
have been involved in sexual
abuse of parishioners. How can
I associate with Christianity?

∥ *Matthew 23:23–33*

The data behind the above assertion is both disturbing
and complicated. An article published in 2010 in *Social
Work and Christianity* (see "For Further Exploration" below) cites wide-ranging, systematic research that asserts
that 3.1 percent of women who attend church services at
least once per month have experienced, at some point
in their lives, sexual advances by a religious leader. This
statistic is both alarming and somewhat reassuring. It is
alarming in that one in thirty-three women has experienced this. It is somewhat reassuring that the numbers
are not even higher.

Yet for those who experience this reality, the impact is
devastating. Particular churches are often more vulnerable than others to this sort of abuse. For example, one
church in West Michigan experienced clergy sexual abuse
by three pastors in a row, with freedom from abuse coming only after the fourth pastor took over. It will be a long
time before churches like that recover from the trauma.

And it is not only women who must endure this sort of abuse, even though they are the primary victims. Children also are victims, sometimes of same-sex abuse as well. The article cited above reports that in 2009, "revelations of clergy sexual abuse of children have cost the U.S. Roman Catholic Church alone more than $2.6 billion since 1950." So, even if this is not that common, the fact that it occurs at all is a serious problem that must be addressed.

Of course, self-centered religious leadership that is more concerned about gratifying its own desires than caring for others is not a new thing. We explored this theme in chapter 7, on the more general failures of religious leaders. Moreover, Matthew 23 contains a chapter-long tirade against the scribes and Pharisees, ancient religious leaders in the practice of Judaism found both in Jesus's day and when Matthew was written. This passage from Matthew does not specifically focus on sexual abuse, but concern about self-centered leadership is clearly present, suggesting that the problem of sexual abuse is expressive of a persistent reality in which religious leaders care more about themselves than about the people they are to lead. For the sake of space, I will not cite the entire chapter, but some verses near the end of Matthew 23 are significant:

> [23] "Woe to you, scribes and Pharisees, hypocrites! For you tithe mint, dill, and cummin, and have neglected the weightier matters of the law: justice and mercy and faith. It is these you ought to have practiced without neglecting the others. [24] You blind guides! You strain out a gnat but swallow a camel!
> [25] "Woe to you, scribes and Pharisees, hypocrites! For you clean the outside of the cup and of the plate,

but inside they are full of greed and self-indulgence.
²⁶ You blind Pharisee! First clean the inside of the cup,
so that the outside also may become clean.

²⁷ "Woe to you, scribes and Pharisees, hypocrites!
For you are like whitewashed tombs, which on the outside look beautiful, but inside they are full of the bones
of the dead and of all kinds of filth. ²⁸ So you also on the
outside look righteous to others, but inside you are full
of hypocrisy and lawlessness.

²⁹ "Woe to you, scribes and Pharisees, hypocrites!
For you build the tombs of the prophets and deco-
rate the graves of the righteous, ³⁰ and you say, 'If we
had lived in the days of our ancestors, we would not
have taken part with them in shedding the blood of
the prophets.' ³¹ Thus you testify against yourselves
that you are descendants of those who murdered the
prophets. ³² Fill up, then, the measure of your ancestors. ³³ You snakes, you brood of vipers! How can you
escape being sentenced to hell?"

These ancient leaders are excoriated because they
"strain out a gnat but swallow a camel" (v. 24). On the
outside they may appear righteous, but inside they are
"full of hypocrisy and lawlessness" (v. 28). In other words,
a concern with a specifically detailed form of righteousness goes hand in hand with abusive behavior. On "little" things, these leaders appear to be rigorous, but in
the big things their behavior is much more problematic.
Hence, it seems evident that the problems of sexual abuse
by Christian leaders today are simply another example
of abusive leadership, which has been around for a very
long time.

This kind of abuse manifests itself in Matthew 23 particularly in economic terms. Matthew 23:16 notes how the scribes and Pharisees insist, "Whoever swears by the sanctuary is bound by nothing, but whoever swears by the gold of the sanctuary is bound by the oath." Later, in verse 18, a similar problem occurs by those who say, "Whoever swears by the altar is bound by nothing, but whoever swears by the gift that is on the altar is bound by the oath." Jesus notes how these distinctions find no basis in the biblical text but conveniently reinforce the obsession with economic issues evident in the scribes and Pharisees.

Nevertheless, in more contemporary times, this obsession with the economic benefit of leaders goes hand in hand with the sexual exploitation of parishioners. In both cases, beneath a veneer of piety lies a deep self-centeredness that sets the values, concerns, and interests of others clearly far below those of the leader. This has always been a recipe for disaster, and still is.

Matthew 23 lays out fairly clear criteria for discerning this problem in leaders. The first criterion is simply consistency between words and actions, both great and small. Consider Matthew 23:23: "Woe to you, scribes and Pharisees, hypocrites! For you tithe mint, dill, and cummin, and have neglected the weightier matters of the law: justice and mercy and faith." Here the problem is obvious: in matters of small details, the scribes and Pharisees pay close attention, but in larger and more comprehensive issues like justice, mercy, and faith, there is a notable absence of concern. The former is easy to objectivize and simple to address; the latter is considerably more complicated, and thus much easier to avoid.

This leads to a second major criterion, related to the

first. It is the issue of proportionality. The smaller and more manageable a particular law is, the easier it is to stay in control. But the bigger and harder to define that issues are, including justice, mercy, and faith, the easier it is to avoid them. Ironically, the smaller an issue is, the easier it is to legislate, but the larger the issue is, the harder legislation becomes.

This leads to a third issue commonly addressed in the Scriptures but not easy to replicate: the role of the prophets. We see this in Matthew 23:29–36, where the scribes and Pharisees honor the prophets from of old but fail to acknowledge the connection the texts imply between them and their ancestors who murdered the prophets. This is particularly difficult in more contemporary times, precisely because of uncertainty about who is, and who is not, a true prophet. Everyone feels free to ignore the words of someone they do not acknowledge as a true prophet, while others may disagree about whether the one speaking is a prophet. But at the very least, the text invites us to pay particular attention when we find ourselves inclined to ignore, or even to physically oppose, those who claim to be speaking for God. Often such people are speaking from the margins, like the prophets from of old, but this makes listening even more challenging but also more important.

The point of all this is that leaders will find elaborate, and sometimes compelling, reasons for us to pay attention to them, and listen to them, despite what they may be doing to contradict their own teaching. We need to cultivate eyes to see and ears to hear those voices at the margins, because it is particularly those voices that most often speak the truth, even though their truth is not guaranteed.

Questions

- How real is this problem in your context?
- What do you make of the claim in this chapter that "in more contemporary times, this obsession with the economic benefit of leaders goes hand in hand with the sexual exploitation of parishioners"?
- What is the relationship between economic abuse and other forms of abuse in your context?
- This chapter suggests that "proportionality" can be a problem in some contexts. Is this a problem in your context?
- Who are the prophets in your context, and how are they recognized?

For Further Exploration

Bruner, Frederick Dale. *Matthew: A Commentary.* Vol. 2, *The Churchbook: Matthew 13–28.* Revised and expanded ed. Grand Rapids: Eerdmans, 2004. Pages 447–52.

Crouch, Andy. *Strong and Weak: Embracing a Life of Love, Risk, and True Flourishing.* Downers Grove, IL: InterVarsity, 2006.

Garland, Diana R., and Christen Argueta. "How Clergy Sexual Misconduct Happens: A Qualitative Study of First-Hand Accounts." *Social Work and Christianity* 37 (2010): 1–28.

12 ∥ Church

*Why should I go to church when
I can just listen to podcasts and go
to a Bible study with friends?*

∥ *Hebrews 10:19–25*

I want to say clearly and unequivocally that listening to podcasts and going to Bible studies with friends are not bad things; they are good things that are to be encouraged. But the question is not whether these things are good or bad; it is whether they are *sufficient* in themselves to be the form of church that characterizes our life.

The answer to that question is no. As valuable as listening to podcasts and doing Bible study with friends may be, they are not fully equivalent to church. These activities are driven by personal preference rather than by the Lordship of Jesus; the primary driver for these decisions is not so much what Jesus wants me to do as what *I* want to do as a follower of Jesus.

That is to say, the focus is *our own* perception of our own personal benefit rather than the one who calls us or the perceptions of outsiders. As such, this way of formulating a decision misses the most common experience of the followers of Jesus, which is that you do not get to choose who else is following Jesus along with you; you simply are required to live with whoever may come along beside you. I can scarcely imagine that the followers of Jesus in the New Testament would have chosen to hang out with tax collectors, prostitutes, and other folks who were disparaged in the general population. Yet the followers of Jesus had no choice in this matter. If they were following Jesus, they had to live with the kinds of people Jesus decided to hang out with.

Here we confront one of the ways in which following Jesus is radically countercultural in our modern context. We are taught, and assume, from early in life, that *what we want* is, and should be, the driver for what we do with our lives. And, as we have already noted, there are corporations that spend billions of dollars making sure that what we want is geared toward their products. So those corporations persist in this emphasis on personal choice and free will, because doing so bolsters their bottom line. But followers of Jesus must necessarily take a radically different perspective on these issues. They recognize that freedom is much harder to come by than our modern world suggests. In fact, what passes for freedom in the eyes of many is merely bondage. And what passes for bondage in the eyes of many is the road to freedom.

What is more significantly lacking in the approach assumed in the opening question is the benefit of listening to others with whom we disagree. It is important to listen not only to our friends but also to our enemies. In fact, Jesus calls us to love our enemies (Matt. 5:44). Jesus notes that if we love only those who love us, we are no better than the gentiles and tax collectors. These are the most noteworthy aspects of friendship that make the question at the beginning of this chapter less than fully adequate. We need to learn to hear from others with whom we disagree.

All this is evident in the key passage for this chapter, Hebrews 10:19–25.

> [19] Therefore, my friends, since we have confidence to enter the sanctuary by the blood of Jesus, [20] by the new and living way that he opened for us through the curtain (that is, through his flesh), [21] and since we have a great priest over the house of God, [22] let us approach with a true heart in full assurance of faith, with our hearts sprinkled clean from an evil conscience and our bodies washed with pure water. [23] Let us hold fast to the confession of our hope without wavering, for he who has promised is faithful. [24] And let us consider how to provoke one another to love and good deeds, [25] not neglecting to meet together, as is the habit of some, but encouraging one another, and all the more as you see the Day approaching.

The passage starts off with this fresh focus: what matters is not what we want, but rather what the blood of Jesus has accomplished for us; it is the blood of Jesus that has opened the sanctuary for us, so that we can enter into the presence of God. It is not our friends or our pious practices that accomplish this; it is done on our behalf by Jesus himself.

As a result, we are invited to discern how to "provoke one another to love and good deeds." The word translated "provoke" in this passage is interesting. In addition to "stirring up" or "provoking," the Bauer Lexicon, a highly respected dictionary of biblical Greek, lists the following other definitions for the word: "sharp disagreement" and "attack of fever" or "convulsion." In other words, this "provoking" of one another is an intense experience, equivalent to an argument or the severe fit of a disease. It does not come "naturally" among friends, but rather pushes us beyond our comfort zones in clear and noticeable ways.

The text goes on to urge its readers not to neglect to meet together, as is the habit of some (v. 25a). In other words, the problem described in the heading of this chapter is not unique, nor is it only a modern problem. Rather, it seems that the writer of Hebrews had to deal with this long ago, when the New Testament was being written. It is never easy to gather with the wide range that makes up the followers of Jesus, even accounting for differences in modern churches over liturgy or styles of worship. We still often experience this impulse to avoid common meetings.

The reason for this emphasis lies in the second half of verse 25, with its invitation to "[encourage] one another, and all the more as you see the Day approaching." This "encouragement" is directly related to the *reconciliation* that marks the life of the church. In other words, if we are only hanging out with folks we already have relationships with and already consider friends, the possibility of this sort of "encouragement" becomes dramatically diminished. "Encouragement" comes specifically from those who are not already in intimate relationships with us. It is these relationships that bear the possibility of significant improvement, and therefore significant encouragement.

Again, the issue is not whether listening to podcasts and going to Bible studies with friends are good. They are. The issue is whether such is enough to fully express our Christian identity, which consistently calls us to move beyond what we find "natural" to embrace a more complex and costly future. Only then will we find that our dependence on Christ is unequivocal and our movement forward is assured.

Discussion Questions

- How important for you is relationship with friends as a central part of Christian faith?
- Do you agree with the claim that listening to podcasts and going to Bible studies with friends are not an adequate expression of Christian faith?
- How much of our Christian faith should be driven by what we want, and how much by our following Jesus?
- What do you make of the discussion of the word "provoke" in this chapter? Is it helpful? How does it speak to your context?
- What do you make of the claim that "encouragement" comes specifically from those who are not already in intimate relationships with us? Do you agree or disagree, and why?

For Further Exploration

Billings, J. Todd. *Remembrance, Communion, and Hope: Rediscovering the Gospel at the Lord's Table*. Grand Rapids: Eerdmans, 2018.

Finney, Mark. "Community." In *The New Interpreter's Dictionary of the Bible*, vol. 1. Nashville: Abingdon, 2006.

Hays, Katie. *We Were Spiritual Refugees: A Story to Help You Believe in Church*. Grand Rapids: Eerdmans, 2020.

Hughes, Philip Edgecumbe. *A Commentary on the Epistle to the Hebrews*. Grand Rapids: Eerdmans, 1977. Pages 405–17.

13 ∥ Women

Why should I trust the "wisdom" of theologians, scholars, and leaders who throughout history have used the Bible to repress women?

∥ 1 Timothy 2:8–12

Let's be clear from the outset: the role of women in most of the history of the church has been fairly severely repressed, for a variety of reasons. Only in the last century have women even begun to be ordained to all the leadership offices of the church. It's also the case that slavery has been accepted through most of the history of the church, and only finally rejected in the middle of the 1800s. So the history of the church is not always a good framework for trying to decide what Christianity or Scripture teaches.

In reality, even today, the issue of women in leadership is an area where Christians differ, and where the church as a whole has respected honest struggle with those differences. Most Christians do not regard people who disagree with them on this issue as heretics, depending on where they stand on it. It's important, therefore, to discuss this issue with respect and a willingness to learn from brothers and sisters in Christ.

While some may simply say that the Bible is out of date and cannot be looked to for authoritative guidance on anything, in most churches, Christians believe that the Bible is our only rule for faith and practice. If a practice isn't biblical, we don't want to do it. For these folks, the debate is not *whether* to be biblical but *how* to be biblical. This is in keeping with an emphasis on the *intention* of Scripture. Interpretation is necessary.

Yet there are several interpretative issues at stake here. First, Christians believe that we need to look at the *whole* of Scripture, not just individual texts. Some more difficult or obscure texts need to be read in the light of the clearer texts, and in light of the message of Scripture as a whole. This is a basic hermeneutical starting point. But we don't always agree on which are the "clear" and which are the "obscure" texts.

We're also dealing in this issue with the complex inter-action between gospel and culture in the New Testament. Christians all agree that both realities are present, but they don't always agree on how to distinguish between the two. Most of us will agree that we are not obligated by Scripture to greet each other with a holy kiss, despite repeated exhortations to this effect (see Rom. 16:16; 1 Cor. 16:20; 2 Cor. 13:12; 1 Thess. 5:26; 1 Pet. 5:14). But we may not be so sure on other texts.

Finally, by way of introduction, most Christians agree that the Bible is authoritative, not because the church says so but by virtue of its witness to Christ. Therefore, all moral or ethical exhortation in Scripture is authoritative only in-sofar as it flows from our life in Christ. It is not enough merely to say "the Bible says so"; we must understand the logic that links particular biblical affirmations or exhorta-tions to life in Christ. Only then will we avoid legalism.

With these preconditions in mind, here are some general observations about women in the Bible that most will agree on: despite the strongly patriarchal character of the Old Testament, women hold some remarkable leadership roles. Miriam, sister of Moses, is described as a prophet (Exod. 15:20). Deborah was a prophet, even described as "judging Israel" (Judg. 4:4–5). Huldah was a prophet consulted on matters of importance to the entire state (2 Kings 22:12–20).

It's also the case that Jesus gave remarkable honor and dignity to women, in a practice that many around him found scandalous. He touched a menstruating woman, forbidden by the Old Testament. He allowed a woman to let her hair down in public and to kiss his feet, a shocking act in that culture. He counted women among his closest followers, and they were present with him at many key junctures in his ministry, including listening to his teaching in the house of Mary and Martha, a place unthinkable in the normal practice of the synagogue. Women were the first witnesses to the resurrection, against the stipulation of the Old Testament that only males are reliable witnesses. Clearly, something radical and dramatic was going on here, central to Jesus's ministry.

Women also exercised remarkable leadership in the early church (though the exact nature of these roles is sometimes disputed). Women were among those included when the eleven met in Jerusalem at the very beginning of the church, even before Pentecost (Acts 1:13–14). Women often hosted churches in their homes: Mary, the mother of John Mark, in Acts 12:12; Lydia, the first convert in Europe and a successful businesswoman, in Acts 16:14–15,

40; as well as the two women, Euodia and Syntyche, in Philippi who appear to play a prominent role (Phil. 4:2–3). Otherwise, why the very public request that they agree? Note that Paul says they "have struggled beside me in the work of the gospel, together with Clement and the rest of my co-workers." We also see Tabitha, "devoted to good works and acts of charity," in Acts 9:36.

Beyond these examples, we also see in the New Testament a variety of other important roles for women: The four daughters of Philip were described as prophetesses (Acts 21:9). Priscilla and her husband, Aquila, were widely known (Rom. 16:3–4) and hosted a local church (1 Cor. 16:19; Rom. 16:5). They give gentle correction to Apollos in his teaching (Acts 18:26). Luke and Paul almost always mention Priscilla first, then Aquila! She is referred to as a "coworker" in Romans 16:4. In addition, a number of women are referred to in Romans 16 as "workers in the Lord": Mary (v. 6), Tryphaena and Tryphosa (v. 12), and Persis (v. 12). Junia in verse 7 is clearly referred to as an "apostle," clearly meaning involved in the proclamation of the gospel and the planting of new churches. Phoebe in 16:1–2 is a *diakonos*, translated "deacon" or perhaps "minister," and Phoebe is referred to in the same text as a *prostatis*, "patron" or "protector."

Thus, however we may apply Galatians 3:28 to the ordination of women, it seems clearly to be standing at the end of the trajectory we have been tracing. Jew and Greek, slave and free, male and female, are all ways in which relationships of superior/inferior, good/bad, and inside/outside had been constructed prior to the writing of this text. But in contrast, Paul insists, "all of you are one in Christ Jesus." The gospel does something fundamental to call all these old divisions into question, including the division of male and female.

But let's also consider a text on the other side, which is commonly used to restrict the freedom and role of women in the church. I'm thinking specifically of 1 Timothy 2:8–12.

> [8] I desire, then, that in every place the men should pray, lifting up holy hands without anger or argument; [9] also that the women should dress themselves modestly and decently in suitable clothing, not with their hair braided, or with gold, pearls, or expensive clothes, [10] but with good works, as is proper for women who profess reverence for God. [11] Let a woman learn in silence with full submission. [12] I permit no woman to teach or to have authority over a man; she is to keep silent.

While there is some debate about this, the overarching context for this passage appears to be public worship rather than advice to individual men and women. This is reflected in the plurals at the beginning and end of the passage, as well as the reference to teaching, which is clearly a public act.

But that raises the problem of verse 12 in particular. In what sense does the writer "permit no woman to teach or to have authority over a man"? The problem is exacerbated by the somewhat rare word for "have authority over" in this text. Is this a neutral reference to authority in the church, or is it a negative reference, equivalent to "boss around"? I think the evidence supports the latter interpretation. (See the essay by Linda L. Belleville in "For

Further Exploration" for more on this.) The alternative of "calmness" (another way to translate "silent") seems to focus not so much on the absence of speech as on composure and peacefulness.

Hence, what is envisioned here is not the normal instruction that takes place in the life of the church; what is in view is a woman "getting in the face" of a man, instructing him what to do in a domineering fashion. It's important to note the switch from plural to singular forms in this verse. While I would not say that only husbands and wives are in view here, the use of singular forms suggests that personal encounters, rather than public teaching, is what is in view.

Much more could be said about this text, as well as the larger context, but what we have focused on suggests that verse 12 in particular is not referring to formal instruction but rather to aggressive encounters between individuals. So this passage doesn't really speak to the issue of the ordination of women in particular, but rather to specific interpersonal conflicts.

We could explore other texts as well, but the pattern is fairly clear. Women and men are urged to get along with each other in the church, and to avoid specific forms of behavior that may, in a particular context, create uncertainty, division, or chaos.

So, rather than imposing a uniform practice differentiated by gender, the pattern in the New Testament is more specific and particular, focusing on healthy interactions between individuals. To return again to the question at the beginning of this chapter: there are plenty of times when men have "used the Bible" to suppress women. But this is hardly what Scripture itself unambiguously teaches, and those who seek to be informed by the whole message of Scripture can find good reasons to develop an alternative that is more affirming to women in leadership in the church. That is the position of this chapter.

Discussion Questions

- Do you agree or disagree with specific claims in this chapter?
- How "disputable" is this question? Can we recognize as Christian those with whom we may disagree on this issue?
- How would you differentiate between gospel and culture in the New Testament on this issue?
- What do you make of the many women in the Bible who seem to be exercising significant leadership?

For Further Exploration

Chaves, Mark. *Ordaining Women: Culture and Conflict in Religious Organizations.* Cambridge, MA: Harvard University Press, 1999.

Grenz, Stanley J., with Denise Muir Kjesbo. *Women in the Church: A Biblical Theology of Women in Ministry.* Downers Grove, IL: InterVarsity, 1995. This is a collection of essays favoring women in leadership.

Grudem, Wayne, and John Piper, eds. *Recovering Biblical Manhood and Womanhood: A Response to Evangel-*

ical Feminism. Wheaton, IL: Crossway, 1991. This is a collection of essays opposing women in leadership.

Pierce, Ronald W., and Rebecca Merrill Groothuis, eds. *Discovering Biblical Equality: Complementarity without Hierarchy*. 2nd ed. Downers Grove, IL: IVP Academic, 2005.

14 ∥ Doubt

I have too many doubts. How can I be a Christian?

∥ *Matthew 14:22–33*

This is a fairly common problem. Particularly in our modern context, people struggle with a rationalistically based alternative to faith that seems to have all the answers. Because (according to this sort of view) everything has a perfectly coherent explanation without appealing to God, appeals to God must be excluded.

But if the text for this chapter (Matt. 14:22–33) has any force at all, the problem of doubt is not merely, or even primarily, a modern problem based in rationalism. Here is the text:

> [22] Immediately he made the disciples get into the boat and go on ahead to the other side, while he dismissed the crowds. [23] And after he had dismissed the crowds, he went up the mountain by himself to pray. When evening came, he was there alone, [24] but by this time the boat, battered by the waves, was far from the land, for the wind was against them. [25] And early in the morning he came walking toward them on the sea. [26] But when the disciples saw him walking on the sea, they were terrified, saying, "It is a ghost!" And they

cried out in fear. [27] But immediately Jesus spoke to them and said, "Take heart, it is I; do not be afraid."

[28] Peter answered him, "Lord, if it is you, command me to come to you on the water." [29] He said, "Come." So Peter got out of the boat, started walking on the water, and came toward Jesus. [30] But when he noticed the strong wind, he became frightened, and beginning to sink, he cried out, "Lord, save me!" [31] Jesus immediately reached out his hand and caught him, saying to him, "You of little faith, why did you doubt?" [32] When they got into the boat, the wind ceased. [33] And those in the boat worshiped him, saying, "Truly you are the Son of God."

In this story, the disciples of Jesus struggle mightily with what they see with their own eyes: Jesus walking on the water. And Peter, of course, pushes the envelope more than any of the others and asks Jesus if he can walk on the water, too. Certainly there is no rationalistic claim here that the rule of gravity is never suspended. But when Jesus answers his request positively and tells him to come out on the water, he eventually becomes terrified and begins to sink in the water, only to be rescued by Jesus himself.

One might suppose that it is a rationalistic move that sinks Peter, but this seems less than probable. For one thing, his life occurs before the rationalistic period of the Enlightenment, so this alone makes this interpretation less likely. But one must also come to grips with the many ways in which Peter's world was upended, even before this event took place. Already, he has seen Jesus heal many people of a variety of diseases and ailments. Already, the disciples have been sent out on their own mission, which included healing the sick, raising the dead, cleansing people of leprosy, and casting out demons (Matt. 10:5–15). The walking on water is not the first time, by any means, that Peter's supposedly rationalistic world has been upended. So when Jesus asks Peter at the end of this passage, "why did you doubt?" in verse 31, rationalism is not a possible explanation. This is a matter of the disciples' attempt to figure out what to expect, in a world where nothing seems predictable at all.

Here we come to the first practical issue for people struggling with doubt. It is important to clarify what is the *source* of the doubt. It may be that claims to miracles disrupt a rationalistic perspective on the world. But it may also be that the world simply seems to be chaotic, and no explanation seems to address all the potential issues that may arise. Clarifying the type of doubt someone is dealing with can often be the first step in addressing the problem.

But clarifying the source or type of doubt does not usually resolve the underlying issue. The underlying issue is that people are inherently cautious about alleged events that run counter to their *experience*, whatever the source and basis of that experience.

What is at stake, then, in addressing the problem of doubt, is helping people to move past the way they have previously understood their experience, helping them to develop a new and different sort of paradigm for interpreting their experience. To do this well requires a lot of listening: How has the person experienced the world in the past, and how does the person interpret that experience? These are not simple questions, and it may take some work and some time to do them justice.

But this is only the beginning, because sooner or later, we will need to confront the issue of divine presence and activity in the world. This problem lies at the core of many experiences of doubt. If there truly is some sort of God, and this God is active and present in the world around us, then all sorts of things are implicated. First, a rationalistic explanation for the phenomena of the world is necessarily transcended. But this is not all. At the opposite end of the spectrum, a random interpretation of experience is equally called into question, at least if there is some purpose to divine activity, which is usually part of the picture. If God is present and active in the world, then things do not happen randomly.

Rather, there is some purpose that underlies what happens in the world. But this, of course, starts to get at the core of doubt from another angle. How do we know what this purpose is, and how do we interpret it? And for many people, this question quickly leads back to the issue of experience: How do I discern any sort of divine presence or action in my own experience?

Here is where the biblical account begins to come into the conversation. Christians commonly appeal to Scripture as the basis for a variety of claims about how God is present in the world. But others will quickly ask why Scripture should be believed in the first place. But it is important, first of all, not to abstract the question of the existence of God from the particular ways in which God is revealed in Scripture. If God really is God, and if Scripture is correct, at least in some sense, in its witness to this reality, then the particularities of the text matter.

But why, in particular, should we regard Scripture as

a correct or accurate portrayal of God? Here we confront the heart of the problem, along with the core of the biblical witness. For at the center of the biblical witness is the notion that God has come to us in Jesus Christ. If this is not true, then nothing else the Bible says means anything to people today. But if it is true, then we know two things in particular: (1) God does in fact exist, and (2) God has come to us uniquely in the person of Jesus Christ.

Here is the core of a response to those who struggle with doubt. One doesn't address doubts in a piece-by-piece rational way, evaluating each claim on its own. One needs to get to the heart of things: Does God exist, and is God revealed in Jesus Christ? Only in this way can we move beyond the paralysis of doubt to some sort of faith. This chapter will not explore how to do this more particularly, but it's important to recognize that this is the path.

Finally, we should say at least a word about the value of doubting. Doubt is not always a bad thing. In fact, it can be the first step in a deeper journey of discovery. Sometimes we need to help people simply to be patient with their doubts and allow the process to take its natural course.

Discussion Questions

- Is doubt a good thing or a bad thing in your context?
- Is the problem with doubt outlined in this essay part of your experience?
- How closely does Matthew 14:22–33 address this problem, and is it helpful?
- Is the way this chapter ends helpful?

For Further Exploration

Broughton, Janet. *Descartes' Method of Doubt.* Princeton: Princeton University Press, 2002.

Stevens, John. *How Can I Be Sure? and Other Questions about Doubt, Assurance, and the Bible.* Surrey, UK: Good Book Co., 2014.

Suk, John. *Not Sure: A Pastor's Journey from Faith to Doubt.* Grand Rapids: Eerdmans, 2011.

Thiselton, Anthony C. *Doubt, Faith, and Certainty.* Grand Rapids: Eerdmans, 2017.

Wennberg, Robert N. *Faith on the Edge.* Grand Rapids: Eerdmans, 2009.

15 ‖ Hell

*If I become a Christian, won't I
need to write off my non-Christian
friends as going to hell?*

‖ *Matthew 25:31–46*

This is a fairly common problem in today's world. Many Christians have acquired a public reputation for judgmentalism, writing off people who disagree with them as going to hell. However, the biblical text is a bit more complicated. Let's look at one of the major texts about final judgment: Matthew 25:31–46:

> [31] "When the Son of Man comes in his glory, and all the angels with him, then he will sit on the throne of his glory. [32] All the nations will be gathered before him, and he will separate people one from another as a shepherd separates the sheep from the goats, [33] and he will put the sheep at his right hand and the goats at the left. [34] Then the king will say to those at his right hand, 'Come, you that are blessed by my Father, inherit the kingdom prepared for you from the foundation of the world; [35] for I was hungry and you gave me food, I was thirsty and you gave me something to drink, I was a stranger and you welcomed me, [36] I was naked and you gave me clothing, I was sick and you took care

of me, I was in prison and you visited me.' ³⁷ Then the
righteous will answer him, 'Lord, when was it that we
saw you hungry and gave you food, or thirsty and gave
you something to drink? ³⁸ And when was it that we
saw you a stranger and welcomed you, or naked and
gave you clothing? ³⁹ And when was it that we saw you
sick or in prison and visited you?' ⁴⁰ And the king will
answer them, 'Truly I tell you, just as you did it to one
of the least of these who are members of my family, you
did it to me.' ⁴¹ Then he will say to those at his left hand,
'You that are accursed, depart from me into the eternal
fire prepared for the devil and his angels; ⁴² for I was
hungry and you gave me no food, I was thirsty and you
gave me nothing to drink, ⁴³ I was a stranger and you
did not welcome me, naked and you did not give me
clothing, sick and in prison and you did not visit me.'
⁴⁴ Then they also will answer, 'Lord, when was it that
we saw you hungry or thirsty or a stranger or naked or
sick or in prison, and did not take care of you?' ⁴⁵ Then
he will answer them, 'Truly I tell you, just as you did
not do it to one of the least of these, you did not do it to
me.' ⁴⁶ And these will go away into eternal punishment,
but the righteous into eternal life."

Multiple issues emerge from this text, but I want to
talk about two in particular. The first concerns the meaning of the word in verse 46 rendered "eternal." At root is
the question about how long final punishment lasts. The
second question has to do with the extent to which going
to hell is *purgative*, with a goal of finishing the cleansing and being brought to heaven, and to what extent it
is *permanent*, indicating a state from which there is no

departure. After we have explored these two questions, we shall return to the more basic question that stands at the beginning of this chapter.

First, the word "eternal." In English, this word has one basic meaning: "without end." Something that is *eternal* never ceases to exist. This meaning was live in the ancient world, too, and is commonly associated with the Greek word that is often translated "eternal." But the Greek word literally means "related to the age." In secular Greek of the period, the word sometimes connotes power related to royalty, particularly imperial royalty in the Roman Empire. Thus the meaning of the word is not always directly related to length of time. It is sometimes more of a qualitative term, raising up the prospect of a very different sort of existence than we experience right now, or underscoring particular aspects of the present context. At stake is a broader distinction between life as we experience it now in "this age" and life as it is experienced in the "age to come."

So while the English word "eternal" always has a temporal connotation, the Greek word from which it is translated here does not. Sometimes it does, but at other times a more qualitative dimension comes to the fore. Of course, if that is the case in our text, then the focus is not on never-ending judgment but on judgment of a particular quality, related to the age to come.

The second question we asked above asks whether going to hell is to be understood as *purgative* or *permanent*. At stake here is the image of *fire*, which goes together with many images of hell and is found in verse 41. This is "the fire prepared for the devil and his angels." And of course, if "eternal" means "unending," then the answer is already evident. But if it does not carry that connotation here, but is simply linked to the coming age, then the issue remains open as to how long this punishment lasts.

A study of the word "fire" in the Old Testament reveals that fire is commonly used as punishment, but the emphasis is consistently on how the fire "consumes" those punished by it. So it is not eternal but very temporal in character, and is irrelevant once it accomplishes its punishing (and consuming) task.

But other New Testament texts tell a slightly different story. Mark 9:43 speaks of hell as having an "unquenchable" fire, suggesting an eternal punishment. Later, in verse 48, Mark cites the final verse of the book of Isaiah, which refers to hell as the place "where . . . the fire is never quenched."

In 1 Corinthians 3:13, by contrast, fire has a purgative and revealing function: "it will be revealed with fire." Set in the context of judgment, this passage speaks about how the truth will be "revealed" by fire. First Corinthians 3:15 is also a key text, which speaks of how, "if the work is burned up, the builder will suffer loss [but] the builder will be saved, but only as through fire." Here the purgative nature of fire is clearly seen.

By contrast, Hebrews 10:27 speaks of a fire that will "consume the adversaries," another destructive image. But on the purgative side, we see 2 Peter 3:12, which states that the "elements" of heaven and earth "will be set ablaze and dissolved," which in the larger context presumes a more purgative notion, where everything will be "disclosed."

Revelation 3:18 speaks of gold that is "refined by fire," suggesting a more purgative notion. Finally, Revelation 20:14–15 speaks of the "lake of fire" as the "second death," suggesting an end (death), not an ongoing punishment.

The evidence is complex and multifaceted. Some passages clearly speak of a "final" judgment as something that "consumes" its victims, after which they will no longer exist. Other passages, such as our text from Matthew 25, speak of "eternal punishment," which, at least in English, conveys the idea of a punishment that has no end but rather causes a continuous suffering. Scholars must decide which is ultimately applicable.

We don't know entirely and clearly whether the judgment allotted to the unrighteous lasts a while or is eternal. But there is an even more important aspect of the Matthew 25 story: both those receiving a positive judgment and those receiving a negative one are surprised by that judgment and don't expect it.

At the very least, that should indicate that we can't predict now what will be the results of the final judgment. Some who think they will be judged positively are mistaken, and some who receive a positive judgment will be surprised. This is an enormously important part of this picture, with respect to Christian identity and church membership. Note that no one in the final judgment is asked whether they are Christian or a member of a church. That is not the issue, and those are not the relevant criteria. The critical issue is how they have responded to the presence of Jesus in those around them.

Some who seem on the inside will end up on the outside, and some who seem on the outside will end up on the inside. That's simply the way it is in this story, which means that we can't make any assumptions about who is going to hell and who is not. So the question with which this chapter begins cannot be answered by us, and is therefore irrelevant. We can't write off our non-Christian friends, because we don't know how they will be treated in the final judgment. Nor can we assume that all who call themselves Christian will receive a positive ruling in the final judgment. All we can do is seek to follow Jesus ourselves as best we can, and leave the rest to God. And that, I believe, is certainly a more positive final place to reside.

Discussion Questions

- How real, in your context, is the problem of hell?
- Is the problem with final judgment outlined in this essay part of your experience?
- How closely does Matthew 25:31–46 address this problem, and is it helpful?
- Is the kind of agnosticism regarding final judgment this chapter advocates helpful or not?

For Further Exploration

Fudge, Edward, and Robert A. Peterson. *Two Views of Hell: A Biblical and Theological Dialogue*. Downers Grove, IL: InterVarsity, 2000.

Runesson, Anders. "Judgment." In *The New Interpreter's Dictionary of the Bible*, vol. 3. Nashville: Abingdon, 2008.

Wilkins, Robert N., Thomas R. Schreiner, James D. G. Dunn, and Michael P. Barber. *Four Views on the Role of Works at the Final Judgment*. Counterpoints. Grand Rapids: Zondervan, 2013.

16 ⫲ Relevance

*Isn't Christianity a fading religion
with shrinking numbers and an
aging population? Why should
I see Christianity as relevant
to anything?*

⫲ Mark 7:1–13

There are two distinct issues here, both of which deserve
our attention in trying to answer this question. The first
issue focuses on whether a minority religion in general
is worth following, or whether one needs to focus on religions that are growing and appealing to younger people. The second issue concerns the extent to which the
assumption that Christianity is a fading religion with
shrinking numbers and an aging population is correct in
the first place.

First question first. Must a religion be growing and
appealing to younger people to be worth following? Right
away, we need to confront the huge change that took
place in Christian faith with the conversion of Constantine in the fourth century. Prior to that time, Christianity
was clearly a minority religion that called into question
basic assumptions about the Roman Empire, a dynamic
we have explored in previous chapters (see especially
chaps. 4 and 9). So, for the first three centuries of its ex-

istence, Christianity was a minority religion. We don't
know how many younger people were part of its makeup,
but as a religion, it clearly did not have overwhelming
numbers to back up its credibility, as the question at the
head of this chapter seems to presuppose.

But is Christianity a growing religion today? According to a 2018 article in the *Guardian*, Christians form the
biggest religious group in the world by some margin, with
2.3 billion adherents, or 31.2 percent of the total world
population of 7.3 billion (for the article, see "For Further
Exploration" below). This article asserts that, while the
median age of the global population is twenty-eight, the
median age for Christians is thirty, placing this group in
a category somewhat older than the general population
(but it may be debatable how significant this statistic is).
Furthermore, the percentage of Christians in the population is declining in much of Europe, particularly among
younger people.

Christianity is still the most adhered-to religion in
the United States, with 75 percent of polled American
adults identifying themselves as Christian in 2015. (This
statistic, from a survey by the Pew Research Center, reflects self-identification and doesn't necessarily entail
church attendance; for the survey, see "For Further Exploration" below.) So, from a strictly statistical perspective, the assumption of this question appears to be at
least somewhat faulty. The statistics simply don't support
the claim that Christianity is a "fading religion" with an
"aging population."

In this context, let's turn to the text that is in focus for
this chapter, Mark 7:1–13:

¹ Now when the Pharisees and some of the scribes who had come from Jerusalem gathered around him, ² they noticed that some of his disciples were eating with defiled hands, that is, without washing them. ³ (For the Pharisees, and all the Jews, do not eat unless they thoroughly wash their hands, thus observing the tradition of the elders; ⁴ and they do not eat anything from the market unless they wash it; and there are also many other traditions that they observe, the washing of cups, pots, and bronze kettles.) ⁵ So the Pharisees and the scribes asked him, "Why do your disciples not live according to the tradition of the elders, but eat with defiled hands?" ⁶ He said to them, "Isaiah prophesied rightly about you hypocrites, as it is written,

> 'This people honors me with their lips,
>   but their hearts are far from me;
> ⁷ in vain do they worship me,
>   teaching human precepts as doctrines.'

⁸ You abandon the commandment of God and hold to human tradition."

⁹ Then he said to them, "You have a fine way of rejecting the commandment of God in order to keep your tradition! ¹⁰ For Moses said, 'Honor your father and your mother'; and, 'Whoever speaks evil of father or mother must surely die.' ¹¹ But you say that if anyone tells father or mother, 'Whatever support you might have had from me is Corban' (that is, an offering to God)— ¹² then you no longer permit doing anything for a father or mother, ¹³ thus making void the word of

God through your tradition that you have handed on.
And you do many things like this."

The key phrase in this text is "the tradition of the elders." What is at stake, of course, is the extent to which
these traditions accurately and helpfully expound the
commandments of God. One of the issues, over which
Jesus disagrees with the interpretation of the scribes and
the Pharisees, has to do with washing. What needs to be
washed, and when, in order to avoid defilement? Jesus
and his disciples interpret the commandment much more
loosely than do the scribes and Pharisees.

But what exactly does the Hebrew Bible say about washing? There are references to washing animals or other food
in Exodus 29:17 and Leviticus 1:9, 13, but I was unable to
find any references to the washing of cooking implements
like cups or bowls. Most of the references to washing in the
Hebrew Bible refer to washing oneself or one's clothes. So
the dispute between Jesus and the scribes and Pharisees
takes place in a sort of vacuum, in which the Hebrew Bible
says little, and people are forced to infer the meaning of
texts that do not speak directly to many circumstances.

So this, more specifically, is what is at stake in this
dispute over the "traditions of the elders." How does one
infer obedience in areas not directly addressed by the
text? Jesus's response has two parts. First, he distinguishes
between what the text actually says and what "the elders"
say the text *means* in a contemporary context. This privileging of "the elders" sometimes amounts to a rejection of
divine authority, both positively and in terms of the limits
of the authority of the text.

This privileging aspect becomes particularly clear in verses 9 and following, where Jesus points out that the "traditions of the elders" are used to avoid more explicit obedience to commands actually found in the text, like the commandment to "honor your father and your mother" in Exodus 20:12. The scribes and Pharisees develop a theology of "Corban" that allows them to avoid direct obedience to an explicit commandment (one of the Ten Commandments). Here is an illustration of a point where the "traditions of the elders" are not so much an attempt to apply the text in a contemporary circumstance not directly addressed by the text itself as a means of avoiding the more direct commandments of Scripture.

But for our purposes in this chapter, what emerges with some clarity is that this concern with the privileging of "the tradition of the elders" has a long history, going back to Jesus himself. There is within Christianity a long-standing objection to doing things "the way we have always done them," and a Christian movement instead to a fresh appropriation of the meaning of the text in our contemporary context.

So, to the extent that the question at the head of this chapter may be true (and there are some significant limits on its truthfulness, as we have already noted), it expresses not something opposed to Christianity but something deeply expressive of Christian faith itself. It is not enough to do things "the way we have always done them." Instead, Jesus calls us to fresh and renewed faithfulness that recognizes the freshness of our context and fails to be bound by patterns from the past. To the extent that we do that, we are following Jesus faithfully.

Discussion Questions

- How important is public success in your context?
- Is the problem with Christianity outlined in this essay part of your experience?
- How closely does Mark 7:1–13 address this problem, and is it helpful?
- Is the approach to tradition this chapter advocates helpful or not?

For Further Exploration

"America's Changing Religious Landscape." Pew Research Center, May 12, 2015. https://www.pewforum.org/2015/05/12/americas-changing-religious-landscape/.

Hays, Katie. *We Were Spiritual Refugees: A Story to Help You Believe in Church*. Grand Rapids: Eerdmans, 2020.

Hobsbawm, Eric, and Terence Ranger, eds. *The Invention of Tradition*. Cambridge: Cambridge University Press, 1983.

Hoogsteen, T. *The Tradition of the Elders: The Way of the Oral Law*. Eugene, OR: Wipf & Stock, 2014.

Sherwood, Harriet. "How Many Believers Are There around the World?" *Guardian*, August 27, 2018. https://www.theguardian.com/news/2018/aug/27/religion-why-is-faith-growing-and-what-happens-next.

Verhey, Allen. *Remembering Jesus: Christian Community, Scripture, and the Moral Life*. Grand Rapids: Eerdmans, 2002. See especially pages 1–76.

17 ⫴ Slavery

What are we to make of the failure
of Christians to consistently favor
the disenfranchised?

⫴ *1 Corinthians 7:21–24*

This is an issue where the problem is fairly self-evident, even though a solution does not seem so clear. Until the middle of the nineteenth century, leading up to the Civil War in the USA, the church had never explicitly said that slavery *as an institution* was morally wrong. In this context, disenfranchised people seemed to have no voice in the church. During the middle of the nineteenth century, this issue may have been ambiguous among some Christian adherents, but at present, virtually all Christians agree that slavery as an institution is morally wrong and that people should not be bought or sold under any circumstances. In this particular sense at least, a concern for the disenfranchised seems to have grown significantly.

But what are we to make of this slow development of a rejection of slavery, in light of the biblical witness? Why did it take almost two thousand years for the church to speak clearly on this issue? Well, we have to say that Scripture itself accounts for some of the ambiguity that we see in the history of the church. There are clearly slaves in the Hebrew Bible. One only needs to think of Hagar, slave to Sarah, the wife of Abraham, in Genesis 16. Later we encounter a whole section concerning slaves and their owners in Exodus 21:1–11. Other examples from the Hebrew Bible could be multiplied.

But the New Testament is not much better on this topic. First Corinthians 7:21–24 seems to suggest that slaves should simply continue in that role: "Were you a slave when called? Do not be concerned about it." A number of other texts in the New Testament seem to presuppose the same reality, including Ephesians 6:5–8 ("Slaves, obey your earthly masters with fear and trembling . . ."), Colossians 3:22–23 ("Slaves, obey your earthly masters in everything . . ."), 1 Timothy 6:1 ("Let all who are under the yoke of slavery regard their masters as worthy of all honor . . ."); see also Titus 2:9–10 and 2 Peter 2:18–22. All these passages seem to presuppose the institution of slavery, and to say nothing against it.

Of course, there are also texts such as Galatians 3:28 and Colossians 3:11 that state that the slave/free distinction does not apply to Christians (Galatians 3:28: "There is no longer Jew or Greek, there is no longer slave or free, there is no longer male and female; for all of you are one in Christ Jesus"). Both the Galatians and the Colossians passages also speak in their context of the distinction between Jew and Greek, and the Galatians text also addresses the male/female distinction as having no significance for Christian identity. Also, texts like Colossians 4:1 ("Masters, treat your slaves justly and fairly, for you know that you also have a Master in heaven") call for a humane approach to slavery, which is helpful but not enough for most modern interpreters.

The central issues emerge in our consideration of a text already cited to some extent: 1 Corinthians 7:21–24:

²¹ Were you a slave when called? Do not be concerned about it. Even if you can gain your freedom, make use of your present condition now more than ever. ²² For whoever was called in the Lord as a slave is a freed person belonging to the Lord, just as whoever was free when called is a slave of Christ. ²³ You were bought with a price; do not become slaves of human masters. ²⁴ In whatever condition you were called, brothers and sisters, there remain with God.

In particular, I want to focus on verse 23, which comes the closest in the canon of Scripture to a more modern perspective: "You were bought with a price; do not become slaves of human masters." Here we see what seems to be the closest thing in the Bible to a theological argument against slavery: there is something incompatible between the radical value that the gospel places on each life and the buying and selling of humans for fixed prices of any sort. Yet we must acknowledge that the New Testament itself does not necessarily draw this conclusion about slavery as an institution. For verse 24 states, "In whatever condition you were called, brothers and sisters, there remain with God." In other words, one should not, according to Paul, *enter into slavery* voluntarily if one does not need to (v. 23), but this is not a categorical rejection of the institution (v. 24). Never do we find in the New Testament an explicit exhortation to do away with the institution of slavery in the culture, despite the qualifying language of some texts such as this one. That would have been far too costly for the church to attempt to do in its ancient context.

In our present context, virtually all Christians agree that slavery as an institution is wrong. The church has completely flipped on this question in the last century and a half. This needs to be explored, however, in the larger context of changing teaching on women in leadership and inclusion of LGBTQIA folk as well. I refer you back to chapter 5, on sexual ethics, for further exploration of these related issues.

Slavery as an institution also presupposes (at least in more modern times) the existence of racism, which is still a problem. It's interesting that the issue of racism was not so closely linked to slavery in the New Testament period. At that time economic issues are what led people into slavery, not so much racial issues. We are not yet done with these economic issues, given financial patterns in this country.

At the same time, note the close link between slavery and racism in the history of the United States. In this context, a darker skin color was a necessary correlate of slavery. And even since slavery as an institution has been eliminated, the persistence of racism based on skin color continues as a serious problem. One gets the sense that the problem of slavery had to get worse before it could even begin to improve. The juxtaposition of racism with slavery may well have provided that further disintegration that forced the issue to be addressed at a more fundamental level, at least with respect to the institution of slavery.

This is enormously important for more conservative exegetes. There are many ways to critique the alliance of racism and slavery that was central to the experience in the United States prior to the Civil War. The Bible speaks against this in multiple ways. So, one doesn't need to engage the ambiguous character of slavery in the New Testament period (which is based much more on economics), since that has a different social function, which is no longer in view in our culture. A simple scan on a topic like "racism and the church" in social media will underscore the extent to which this tends to be the focus of a discussion of slavery in more contemporary conservative contexts.

At the same time, we still face the problem of the powerless and disenfranchised who still suffer, despite the elimination of the institution of slavery. Here we see the flip side of this conversation. One can so closely link slavery and racism that it is far too easy to assume that once slavery is addressed, one does not need to further address the sin of racism, since that issue is already addressed under the rubric of slavery. Rather, we do better to recognize the similar motives underlying *both* slavery and racism in our modern context, and to do our best to eliminate both of them.

Discussion Questions

- How closely are slavery and racism aligned in your context and experience?
- What are we to make of the economic form of slavery that was common in the context of the Roman Empire and the writing of the New Testament? Do these issues still confront us?
- What are we to make of the failure of the Bible to speak clearly and unequivocally against slavery? Is this a problem?
- Is slavery a problem only insofar as it intersects with racism, or are there other issues we must address as well?

- What about racism in its own right? To what extent should the church address this issue?

For Further Exploration

Bales, Kevin. *Disposable People: New Slavery in the Global Economy.* 3rd ed. Berkeley: University of California Press, 2012.

Fitzmyer, Joseph A. *First Corinthians: A New Translation with Introduction and Commentary.* Anchor Yale Bible. New Haven: Yale University Press, 2008. Pages 305–11.

Parish, Peter J. *Slavery: History and Historians.* London: Routledge, 2018.

Tisby, Jemar. *The Color of Compromise: The Truth about the American Church's Complicity in Racism.* Grand Rapids: Zondervan, 2019.

Conclusion

It is hard to know what to put in a conclusion for this book. Certainly, each of these chapters raises a host of issues. How does one bring this to a conclusion? Perhaps the first step is to realize that there is no single conclusion. Rather, the critical issue is the directions that this book leads one to pursue, and the clarity with which one pursues those directions.

Furthermore, I want to emphasize again that this book does not provide comprehensive answers to the questions at the beginning of the chapters. Rather, I have tried to see how a particular text of Scripture reframes, refocuses, but also at least partially answers each question. This is part of my identity as a New Testament scholar. I'm not trying to cover everything; I am simply trying to let the New Testament speak to some contemporary issues with greater clarity.

At the same time, it is central to find the right "angle of approach" to these questions. Learning how to ask the right questions, and how to push in the right direction for answers to those questions, is absolutely central, and that is the focus of this book. Particularly when we consult with younger people, the first step is to learn to ask the right questions of them, and to ask them in the right way.

If this book contributes to long conversations with those we love, I will consider it a success.

Finally, I want to say a word about the people involved. This book was written, first of all, to address common questions raised by younger people. I did quite a bit of survey work early on in the process of developing this book to make sure that the questions had this sort of integrity. But this book is also written for people who are close to those asking the questions. In that sense, reading many of these chapters is an act of service for others whom we love.

Index